STANDOUT

LITERACY FOUNDATIONS

ROB JENKINS

STACI JOHNSON

Australia • Brazil • Canada • Mexico • Singapore • United Kingdom • United States

National Geographic Learning,
a Cengage Company

Stand Out: Literacy Foundations
Rob Jenkins, Staci Johnson

Publisher: Sherrise Roehr

Executive Editor: Sarah Kenney

Senior Development Editor: Margarita Matte

Director of Global Marketing: Ian Martin

Heads of Regional Marketing:

 Charlotte Ellis (Europe, Middle East and Africa)

 Justin Kaley (Asia and Greater China)

 Irina Pereyra (Latin America)

 Joy MacFarland (US and Canada)

Senior Content Project Manager: Beth McNally

Senior Media Researcher: Leila Hishmeh

Senior Art Director: Brenda Carmichael

Operations Support: Hayley Chwazik-Gee,
Katie Lee

Manufacturing Buyer: Terrence Isabella

Composition: MPS North America LLC

For permission to use material from this text or product,
submit all requests online at **cengage.com/permissions**
Further permissions questions can be emailed to
permissionrequest@cengage.com

Student's Book
ISBN: 978-0-357-96467-5
Student's Book with the Spark platform
ISBN: 978-0-357-96466-8

National Geographic Learning
5191 Natorp Blvd, Mason, OH 45040
USA

Locate your local office at **international.cengage.com/region**

Visit National Geographic Learning online at **ELTNGL.com**
Visit our corporate website at **www.cengage.com**

Printed in China
Print Number: 01 Print Year: 2023

Acknowledgments

Mai Ackerman
Ventura College; Los Angeles Mission College, CA

Raul Adalpe
Tarrant County College, Paradise, TX

Mariam Aintablian
Los Angeles Valley College, Valley Glen, CA

Steven Amos
Norfolk Public Schools/Adult Education Services, VA

Ana Arieli
College of Southern Nevada, Las Vegas, NV

Rachel Baiyor
Literacy Outreach, Glenwood Springs, CO

Gregory Baranoff
Santa Barbara City College, Santa Barbara, CA

Valerie Bare
Chesterfield County Public Schools, VA

Dyani Bartlett
Edmonds College, Lynnwood, WA

Karin Bates
Immigrant and Refugee Center of Northern Colorado, CO

Robin Bitters
Adult Learning Program, Jamaica Plain Community Center, Boston, MA

Emily Bryson
ELT Specialist, Author, Teacher, Teacher Trainer, Graphic Facilitator, ESOL Lecturer

Janelle Cardenas
Tarrant County College, TX

Joyce Clement
Chesterfield County Public Schools, VA

Juan Corona
Antelope Valley Adult School, Palmdale, CA

Vasilika Culaku
Goodwill, King County, Seattle, WA

Melinda Dart
Chesterfield County Public Schools, VA

Lourdes Davenport
Tarrant County College, TX

Geisa Dennis
Orange County Public Schools, Orlando, FL

Katie Donoviel
English Skills Learning Center, UT

Reyye Esat Yalcin
Bilingual Education Institute, Houston, TX

Aimee Finley
Dallas College, Dallas, TX

Eleanor Forfang-Brockman
Tarrant County College, Fort Worth, TX

Martha Fredendall
Literacy Outreach, Glenwood Springs, CO

Maria Gutierrez
Miami Sunset Adult Education Center, Miami, FL

Anne Henderson
Goodwill, King County, Seattle, WA

Tracey Higgins
Edmonds College, Lynnwood, WA

Daniel Hopkins
Tarrant County College, TX

Fayne Johnson
Atlantic Technical College, Arthur Ashe Jr. Campus, Fort Lauderdale, FL

Angela Kosmas
City Colleges of Chicago, Chicago, IL

John Kruse
University of Maryland, Arnold, MD

Neskys Liriano
New York Mets, Port Saint Lucie, FL

Maria Manikoth
Snohomish County Goodwill Job Training and Education Center, Everett, WA

Sean McCroskey
Goodwill, King County, Seattle, WA

Yvonne McMahon
Houston Community College, Houston, TX

Sarah Moussavi
Chaffey College, Rancho Cucamonga, CA

Xavier Munoz
Literacy Council of Northern Virginia, Falls Church, VA

Luba Nesterova
Bilingual Education Institute, Houston, TX

Melody Nguyen
Tarrant County College, Arlington, TX

Joseph Ntumba
Goodwill, King County, Seattle, WA

Sachiko Oates
Santa Barbara City College, Santa Barbara, CA

Liane Okamitsu
McKinley Community School for Adults, Honolulu, HI

Dana Orozco
Sweetwater Union High School District, Chula Vista, CA

Betty Osako
McKinley Community School for Adults, Honolulu, HI

Dr. Sergei Paromchik
Adult Education Hillsborough County Public Schools, Tampa, FL

Ileana Perez
Robert Morgan Tech. College, Miami, FL

Carina Raetz
Academy School District 20, Colorado Springs, CO

Tom Randolph
Notre Dame Education Center, Lawrence, MA

Jody Roy
Notre Dame Education Center, Lawrence, MA

Andrew Sansone
Families for Literacy, Saint Peter's University, Jersey City, NJ

Lea Schultz
Lompoc Adult School and Career Center, Lompoc, CA

Jenny Siegfried
Waubonsee Community College, Aurora, IL

Daina Smudrins
Shoreline Community College, Shoreline, WA

Stephanie Sommers
Minneapolis Adult Education, Robbinsdale, MN

Bonnie Taylor
Genesis Center, RI

Yinebeb T. Tessema
Goodwill, King County, Seattle, WA

Dr. Jacqueline Torres
South Dade Senior High, Homestead, FL

Cristina Urena
Atlantic Technical College, Coconut Creek, FL

Marcos Valle
Edmonds College, Lynnwood, WA

Ricardo Vieira Stanton
Bilingual Education Institute, Houston, TX

Lauren Wilson
Shoreline Community College, Shoreline, WA

Pamela Wilson
Palm Beach County Adult and Community Education, FL

ROB JENKINS

STACI JOHNSON

We believe that there's nothing more incredible than the exchange of teaching and learning that goes on in an ESL classroom. And seeing the expression on a student's face when the light goes on reminds us that there's nothing more rewarding than helping a student succeed.

Throughout our careers, we have watched as students rise to challenges and succeed where they were not sure success was possible. Seeing their confidence grow and skills develop brings great joy to both of us and it motivates us to find better ways to reach and support them. We are humbled to think that our contributions to the field over the last 20 years have made a small difference in both students' and teachers' lives. We hope our refinements in ongoing editions will further support their growth and success.

At its core, **Stand Out** has always prioritized robust, relevant content that will deliver student gains in the classroom; while that core mission has not changed, how the program achieves it has certainly evolved in response to a changing educational landscape. The basic principles that have made **Stand Out** successful have not changed. Students are challenged to collaborate and think critically through a well-organized series of scaffolded activities that lead to student application in each lesson. The popular first-of-their-kind lesson plans are still prominent. Features such as project-based learning, video, online practice, multilevel worksheets, and classroom presentation tools continue to support the core series. New to the fourth edition is explicit workplace exploration. A lesson in each unit has been added to explore different fields and careers, potential salaries, skills, and characteristics that workers might have to excel in potential jobs. Also new to the fourth edition, students will be introduced to *Life Online* in tips, activities, and videos throughout the series. In addition, **Stand Out** will now be available in different digital formats compatible with different devices. Finally, **Stand Out** introduces a literacy level that will give access through a unique systematic approach to students who struggle to participate. We believe that with these innovations and features the fourth edition will bring success to every student.

STAND OUT MISSION STATEMENT

Our goal is to inspire students through challenging opportunities to be successful in their language learning experience so they develop confidence and become independent lifelong learners, preparing them for work, school, and life.

Scope and Sequence

UNIT	LESSON 1	LESSON 2	LESSON 3
PRE-UNIT **Welcome** *Page 2*	Alphabet Greetings	Numbers 0–9 Phone numbers	Classroom instructions

Life Online Video: Am I a Letter?

1 **Personal Information** *Page 22*	First and last name **Letter:** Upper and lowercase **n** **Words:** name	Greeting cards Introductions **Letter:** Upper and lowercase **h** **Words:** happy	Address **Letter:** Upper and lowercase **(wh) w** **Words:** where, what
2 **The Classroom** *Page 54*	Introductions **Letter:** Upper and lowercase **f, fr, fl** **Words:** friend	Classroom instructions **Letter:** Upper and lowercase **p** **Words:** please	My classroom **Letter:** Upper and lowercase **c, ck** **Words:** on, in
3 **Food** *Page 86*	Shopping **Letter:** Upper and lowercase **b** **Words:** buy, like	Shopping list **Letter:** Upper and lowercase **ch** **Words:** need	Restaurant **Letter:** Upper and lowercase **s** **Words:** and

Nationality	Family relationships	Review
Letter: Upper and lowercase **m**	**Letter:** Upper and lowercase **r**	**Letter:** Upper and lowercase **a** (*cat*)
Words: from	**Words:** this	**Words:** live, first, last

Schedules / Times	Calendar / Days of the week	Review
Letter: Upper and lowercase **s**	**Letter:** Upper and lowercase **d**	**Letter:** Upper and lowercase **a** (*day*)
Words: at	**Words:** my, your	**Words:** go, school, you

Recipe	Meals	Review
Letter: Upper and lowercase **k**	**Letter:** Upper and lowercase **l**	**Letter:** Upper and lowercase **e**, **ea**, **ee**
Words: want	**Words:** for, eat	**Words:** meal, cook, cut

Scope and Sequence

LESSON 4	LESSON 5	LESSON 6
Sizes	Ads / Prices	Review
Letter: Upper and lowercase **e** (*extra*)	**Letter:** Upper and lowercase **v**	**Letter:** Upper and lowercase **a**
Words: small, large	**Words:** how, much	**Words:** the, wearing
Housing	Housing ads	Review
Letter: Upper and lowercase **y** (*happy*)	**Letter:** Upper and lowercase **th** (*three*)	**Letter:** Lowercase **ou**
Words: yes, no	**Words:** with	**Words:** have, has
Doctor's office	Medicine	Review
Letter: Lowercase **-ing**	**Letter:** Upper and lowercase **i** (*pill*)	**Letter:** Lowercase long vowels
Words: who, next	**Words:** some, take	**Words:** am, are, is

Scope and Sequence

	LESSON 4	LESSON 5	LESSON 6
	Following instructions	Evaluations	Review
	Letter: Upper and lowercase **g**	**Letter:** Upper and lowercase **o** (*hot*)	**Letter:** Upper and lowercase **j**
	Words: big, job	**Words:** good, comes	**Words:** don't, doesn't
	Educational plans	Goals	Review
	Vowels and schwa	**Review:** *c, ch, s, sh*	**Review:** *er, or, ur, u, g, o, j*
	Words: then, right	**Words:** plans, now, will	

spark

Bring *Stand Out* to life with the Spark platform — where you can prepare, teach, and assess your classes all in one place!

Manage your course and teach great classes with integrated digital teaching and learning tools. Spark brings together everything you need on an all-in-one platform with a single log-in.

Track student and class performance on independent online practice and assessment, including CASAS practice. The Course Gradebook helps you turn information into insights to make the most of valuable classroom time.

Set up classes and roster students quickly and easily on Spark. Seamless integration options and point-of-use support helps you focus on what matters most: student success.

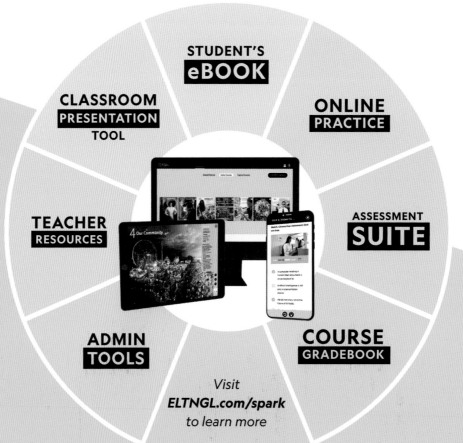

STUDENT'S eBOOK

CLASSROOM PRESENTATION TOOL

ONLINE PRACTICE

TEACHER RESOURCES

ASSESSMENT SUITE

ADMIN TOOLS

COURSE GRADEBOOK

Visit
ELTNGL.com/spark
to learn more

Welcome

Teacher Notes

Use this picture to help show students they are probably already decoding written text to some extent. Say:

Point to a number.   Point to the color red.   Point to the color blue.   Point to the score. Who is winning?

What's Your Name? The alphabet

Hi, I'm Hanah.

H-a-n-a-h.

Nice to meet you.

Teacher Notes

A Listen and repeat.

Aa   Bb   Cc   Dd   Ee
Ff   Gg   Hh   Ii   Jj
Kk   Ll   Mm   Nn   Oo
Pp   Qq   Rr   Ss   Tt
Uu   Vv   Ww   Xx   Yy
Zz

C

A...B...C...D

Teacher Notes

B Listen and repeat.   C Play the disappearing alphabet game. Write the entire alphabet on the board. Erase a letter. Students say the entire alphabet. Erase another letter, then two. How long can they continue?

A	g
D	z
G	a
H	w
M	r
N	m
R	d
S	h
W	n
Z	s

Teacher Notes

D Match the uppercase letter to the lowercase letter.

E ✏️

F ✏️

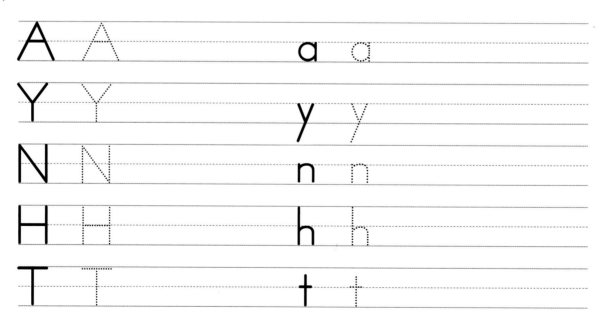

Teacher Notes

E Write.   **F** Trace the letters. Then write the letters again.

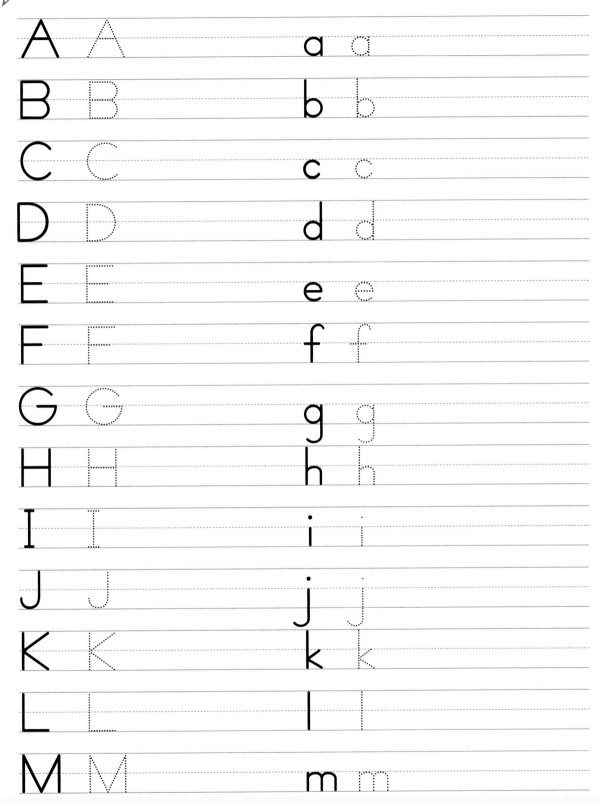

Teacher Notes

G Trace the letters. Then write the letters again.

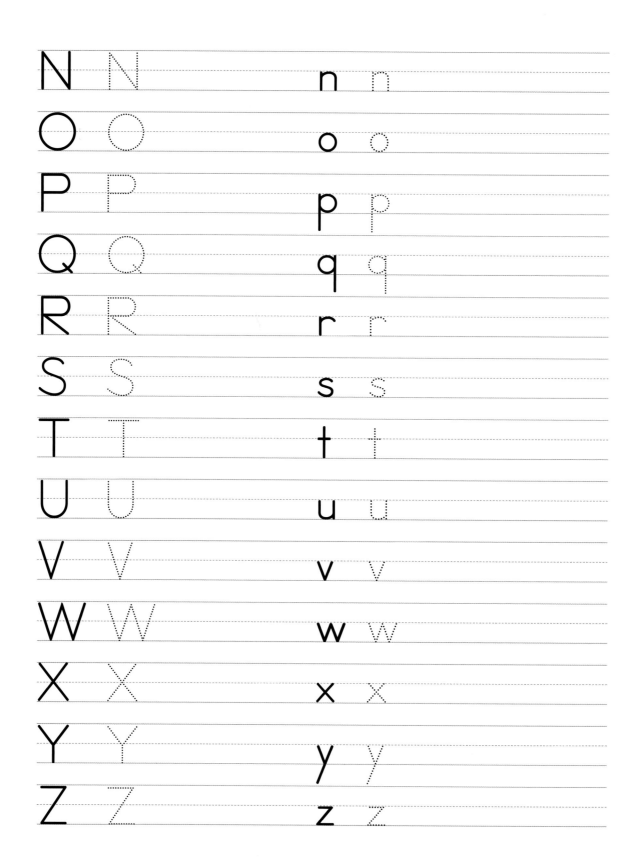

Teacher Notes

G Trace the letters. Then write the letters again.

My name is Hanah. What's your name?

Ana. A-n-a.

Ana   Beto   Carlo   Damsa

Teacher Notes

H Listen and repeat.   I Write your name four times.   J Ask students to line up in alphabetical order by first name.

2 What's Your Number? Numbers 0-9

Teacher Notes

A Listen and repeat. Practice phone numbers using the picture.

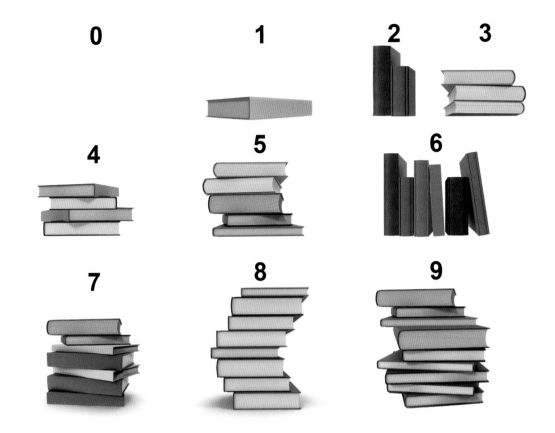

| **0** | | **1** | | **2** | **3** |

	0	**1**	**2**	**3**	**4**	**5**	**6**	**7**	**8**	**9**
a.	0	1	2	3	4	(5)	6	7	8	9
b.	0	1	2	3	4	5	6	7	8	9
c.	0	1	2	3	4	5	6	7	8	9
d.	0	1	2	3	4	5	6	7	8	9
e.	0	1	2	3	4	5	6	7	8	9

Teacher Notes

B Listen and repeat.   **C** Listen and circle the number you hear.

D

0 1 2 3 4 5 6 7 8 9

E

Teacher Notes

D Trace. Write the numbers.　　**E** Count. Write the numbers.

12 twelve

F 🎧 ✏️ 🗣️

a. 7 1 4 – 5 5 5 – 3 7 _3_ 9

b. 4 6 9 – 5 5 5 – ___ 0 6 6

c. 2 1 2 – 5 5 5 – 1 5 7 ___   **4 = 4**

d. 7 8 6 – 5 5 5 – 3 ___ 8 6

e. 8 1 8 – 5 5 5 – 3 7 5 ___

My number is 714-555-3739.

G ✏️

_____
_____
_____
_____
_____

H 🗣️🗣️

3

Teacher Notes

F Listen. Write the number. Repeat.   **G** Write your phone number two times.

H Play a number guessing game.

3 **Follow Instructions** Instructions

Open your books, please.

Open

Close

1. Open your books to page 175, 1-7-5.

2. Open your books to page 33, 3-3.

3. Close your books.

 C

Listen. **Repeat.** **Write.** **Practice.**

 D

1.	a.	(b.)	c.
2.	a.	b.	c.
3.	a.	b.	c.
4.	a.	b.	c.
5.	a.	b.	c.
6.	a.	b.	c.
7.	a.	b.	c.
8.	a.	b.	c.

Teacher Notes

C Listen and repeat.   D Listen and circle the correct answer.

 **E**

Underline. **Circle.** **Check.**

 F

1. Listen   ··

2. Repeat

3. Write

4. Underline

5. Circle

6. Check

 G

Teacher Notes

E Listen and repeat.   **F** Listen and match.   **G** Play. Listen. Practice. Hold up the word / notecard.

A: Please spell your name.

B: A-m-a-d.

A: Please spell your name.

B: _____

Teacher Notes

H Listen and repeat.   **I** Listen. Repeat.   **J** Practice. Spell your name.

seventeen   **17**

Quiz

A 🖉

B 🖉

C

1.	a. 🔊👂	b. ABC✓	c. 📖
2.	a. ___🖉	b. 🗣️	c. ⊘🖉
3.	a. ✓	b. 🗣️	c. 🖉
4.	a. 📖	b. 🗣️	c. 📕
5.	a. ABC✓	b. ___🖉	c. 🔊👂

Teacher Notes

A Write your name.　　**B** Write your phone number.　　**C** Listen and circle.

18　eighteen

Bingo

Teacher Notes

A Write or draw a word for each square. Listen. Play.
(Word list: listen, repeat, write, underline, circle, check, spell, practice, name.) The first student who gets three in a row wins.

Am I a Letter?

A 🖉

A B C D ____ F G H I J K L ____

N O ____ Q R S T U V W X Y ____

B 🖉

____ b c d e f g h ____ j k l m

n o p q r ____ t u v w ____ y z

C 🖉

0 ____ 2 3 ____ 5 6 ____ 8 9

Teacher Notes

A Write the missing uppercase letters.　**B** Write the missing lowercase letters.　**C** Write the missing numbers.

D

Am I a letter?

1. 9   P

2. E   3

3. S $

4. α   @

5. !   i

a = α

E ✓

F

al@mail.com   al at mail dot com

han@here.edu   han at here dot edu

val@mail.com   val at mail dot com

| Email: | name | @ | mail | dot | com |

G

Name: _____

Email: _____

Password: _____

Teacher Notes

D Circle the letters.   **E** Watch the video and check answers in **D**.   **F** Listen and repeat the email addresses.

G On a separate piece of paper, have students write their login credentials.

1 Personal Information

Teacher Notes

Point to the cell phone.   Point to the address.

Point to the driver's license.

1 What's Your Name? n

A Listen. Repeat. n n n n

B Listen. Repeat.

NEW ADULT SCHOOL
School Application
First name: *Neda* Last name: *Mendoza*
Phone number: *714-723-9999*

C Listen. Circle.

1. (a.)   b.   c.

2. a.   b.   c.
   01234
   56789

3. a. 911   b.   c.

4. a.   b.   c.

Teacher Notes

A Listen and repeat the *n* sound.   **B** Listen and repeat.   **C** Listen and circle words that begin with *n*.

D Circle.

n	m	(n)	n	m	n	m	m	n
n	n	h	n	m	h	n	m	n
n	h	n	n	n	m	u	n	n

E Write *n*.

n   n n n n n n n n n n n

n n n n n n n n n n n

n

n

F Listen. Repeat. Write *n*.

1. __n__ame

7 8 9 2. _____umbers

3. _____urse

4. _____otepad

Teacher Notes

D Circle the letter *n*.   **E** Write *n*.   **F** Listen. Repeat. Write *n*.

G Write *N.* 🖉

N N N N N N N N N N

N N N N N N N N N N

N

N

H Listen. 👂 Repeat. 🗣 Write *N.* 🖉

Her name is **N**ancy.

His name is **N**ate.

Her name is _____ancy.

His name is _____ate.

Teacher Notes

G Write *N.*   **H** Listen. Repeat. Write *N.*

I Listen. Repeat.

Hello. My name is <u>Nuan</u>.

name

Nice to meet you. My name is <u>Niu</u>.

J Practice.

K Listen. Repeat.

A: What is your last name?

B: Kang. K-a-n-g.

NEW ADULT SCHOOL
School Application

First name: *Neda*   **Last name:** *Mendoza*

Phone number: *714-723-9999*

L Practice.

M Write *name.*

name

N Listen. Repeat.

A: Spell *name.*

B: n…a…m…e

Teacher Notes

I Listen and repeat.   **J** Practice the conversation in pairs.   **K** Listen and repeat.
L Practice the conversation. Line up by last name.   **M** Write *name.*   **N** Listen and repeat.

twenty-seven   **27**

O Listen. 🦻 Look. 👁

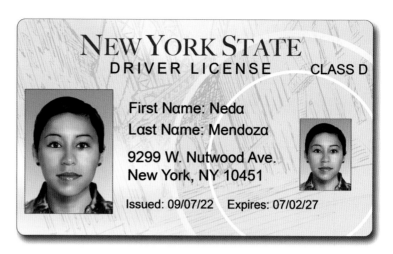

NEW YORK STATE
DRIVER LICENSE   CLASS D

First Name: Neda
Last Name: Mendoza

9299 W. Nutwood Ave.
New York, NY 10451

Issued: 09/07/22   Expires: 07/02/27

P Underline *N* and *n*. ✏️   Circle *name*. ✏️

Q Listen. 🦻 Circle. ✏️

1. What is her first name?   a. Neda   b. Mendoza

2. What is her last name?   a. Mendoza   b. Nutwood

R Write. ✏️

Student ID
First name:
Last name:
Phone number:

Teacher Notes

O Listen. Track the words. Point to the look icon and word. Explain that it means to follow the words in the text.
P Underline *N* and *n*. Circle *Name*.   **Q** Listen and circle the answer.   **R** Write your information.

28   twenty-eight

2 Hello! h

A Listen. Repeat.

h   h   h   h

B Listen. Repeat.

C Listen. Circle.

1. a.   b.   c.

2. a.   b.   c.

3. a.   b.   c.

4. a.   b.   c.

Teacher Notes

A Listen and repeat the *h* sound.   **B** Listen and repeat.   **C** Listen and circle words that begin with *h*.

D Circle. ✏️

h	n	(h)	n	n	h	h	n	n
h	b	h	h	n	n	ḍ	h	ḍ
h	ḍ	h	b	n	h	n	b	ḍ

E Write h. ✏️

F Listen. 👂 Repeat. 🗣️ Write h. ✏️

 1. __h__appy

 2. _____at

 3. _____ead

 4. _____ello

Teacher Notes

D Circle h.　　**E** Write h.　　**F** Listen and repeat. Write h.

G Write *H*.

H H H H H H H H H H

H H H H H H H H H

H

H

H Listen. 🖎 Repeat. 🗣 Write *H*. ✏

Happy Birthday!

____appy Birthday!

Harry and **H**anna

____arry and ____anna

Teacher Notes

G Write *H*.   **H** Listen and repeat. Write *H*.

thirty-one   **31**

I Listen. Repeat. Practice.

Hello! I'm Henry.

Hi. I'm Zahir.

J Listen. Repeat. Practice.

A: Happy to meet you, <u>Henry</u>.

B: I am happy to meet you, too.

happy

K Write *happy*.

happy

L Listen. Repeat.

A: Spell *happy*.　　　**A:** Spell *name*.

B: h…a…p…p…y　　　**B:** n…a…m…e

M Spell.

Teacher Notes

I Listen and repeat. Then practice the conversation in pairs. **J** Listen and repeat. Then practice the conversation. Memorize as many names as you can. **K** Write *happy*. **L** Spell *happy* and *name*. **M** Spell. Make words.

N Listen. Look.

O Underline *H* and *h*. Circle *happy*.

P Listen. Circle.

1. Who is the card to?　　　a. Harry　　b. Zahir
2. Who is the card from?　　a. Harry　　b. Zahir

Q Write.

> Dear Teacher,
>
> Thank you for the class. I am happy!
>
> Your student, _____

R Write.

_____

_____

_____

Teacher Notes

N Listen and repeat. Track the words.　　**O** Underline *H* and *h* in the thank you card. Circle *happy*.

P Listen and circle the answer.　　**Q** Write *Thank You*. Then have students write their names.

R Write a Thank You card.

3 Where Do You Live?   (wh) w

A **Listen.** **Repeat.**

w   w   w   w

B **Listen.** **Repeat.**

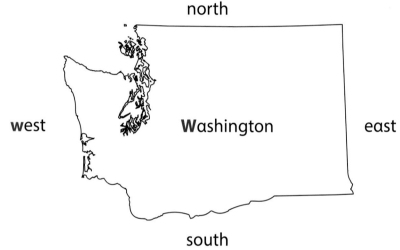

north

west   **W**ashington   east

south

C **Listen.** **Circle.**

1. a. ⬛   b. 🧭   c. 🗺️

2. a. 📓   b.   c. 🚗

3. a. 🚌   b. ⬛   c. ⊞

4. a.   b.   c. 🎧

Teacher Notes

A Listen and repeat the *w* sound.   **B** Listen and repeat.   **C** Listen and circle words that begin with *w*.

D Circle. 🖊

w	v	ⓦ	v	m	v	w	w	w
w	w	v	u	m	v	w	u	w
w	u	w	3	m	w	v	w	u

E Write *w*. 🖊

W   W   W   W   W   W   W   W   W   W

W   W   W   W   W   W   W   W   W   W

W

W

F Listen. 👂   Repeat. 🗣   Write *w*. 🖊

 1. __w__est

  2. _____ater

 3. _____all

4. _____indow

Teacher Notes

D Circle *w*.   **E** Write *w*.   **F** Listen and repeat. Write *w*.

G Write *W*.

W W W W W W W W
W W W W W W W W
W
W

H Listen. Repeat. Write *W*.

Where do you live?

_____here do you live?

What is your address?

_____hat is your address?

Teacher Notes

G Write *W*.   **H** Listen and repeat. Write *W*.

36   thirty-six

I Listen. Repeat.

A: Where do you live?

B: Seattle, Washington.

where
what

J Practice.

K Listen. Repeat. Practice.

What is your address?   1123 West Arnell Street.

L Write *where* and *what*.

where

what

M Spell.

Teacher Notes

I Listen and repeat.   **J** Practice the conversation.   **K** Listen and repeat. Practice the conversation.

L Write *where* and *what*.   **M** Spell words with alphabet cards.

N Listen. Repeat.

A: Spell *where*. **A:** Spell *what*. **A:** Spell *happy*. **A:** Spell *name*.

B: w…h…e…r…e **B:** w…h…a…t **B:** h…a…p…p…y **B:** n…a…m…e

O Listen. Repeat.

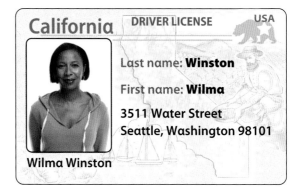

California DRIVER LICENSE USA

Last name: **Winston**
First name: **Wilma**

3511 Water Street
Seattle, Washington 98101

Wilma Winston

P Underline *W*.

Q Listen. Circle.

1. What is her first name?   a. Winston   b. Wilma

2. Where does she live?   a. Seattle   b. Winston

R Write.

Driver License		
First name: _____		
Last name: _____		
Address: _____		
_____		

Teacher Notes

N Practice spelling in pairs. Spell *where, what, happy,* and *name*.   **O** Listen and repeat. Track the text.
P Underline *W*.   **Q** Listen. Circle the answer.   **R** Write your information.

4 Where Are You From? m

A Listen. Repeat.

m m m m

B Listen. Repeat.

Map of Mexico

I'm from Mexico City, Mexico.

Mexico

Mexico City

C Listen. Circle.

1. (a.) 　　b. 　　c.

2. a. 　　b. 　　c.

3. a. 　　b. 　　c.

4. a. 　　b. 　　c.

Teacher Notes

A Listen and repeat the *m* sound.　　**B** Listen and repeat.　　**C** Listen and circle words that begin with *m*.

D Circle.

m	w	w	(m)	m	m	w	m	w
m	n	m	m	n	w	n	m	w
m	m	m	n	n	m	w	n	n

E Write m.

m   m   m   m   m   m   m   m   m

m   m   m   m   m   m   m   m   m

m

m

F Listen. Repeat. Write m.

 1. _m_ap

 2. na____e

 3. ____ask

 4. ____oney

 5. ____an

 5. wo____an

Teacher Notes

D Circle m.   **E** Write m.   **F** Listen and repeat. Write m.

G Write *M.* ✏️

M M M M M M M M M
M M M M M M M M M
M
M

H Listen. 👂) Repeat. 🗣 Write *M.* ✏️

Maria

_____aria

Masks are required.

_____asks are required.

Teacher Notes

G Write *M.*   **H** Listen and repeat. Write *M.*

I Listen. 🔊 **Repeat.** 🗣️

A: What is your name?

B: I'm Maria, M...a...r...i...a.

A: Where are you from?

B: I'm from Mexico, M...e...x...i...c...o.

from

J Practice. 🗣️🗣️

K Write *from.* ✏️

from

L Listen. 🔊 **Repeat.** 🗣️

A: Spell *from.*

B: f...r...o...m

A: Spell *where.*

B: w...h...e...r...e

A: Spell *what.*

B: w...h...a...t

A: Spell *happy.*

B: h...a...p...p...y

A: Spell *name.*

B: n...a...m...e

M Practice. 🗣️🗣️

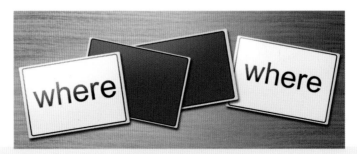

Teacher Notes

i Listen and repeat.   **J** Practice the conversation with your information.   **K** Write *from.*

L Spell *from, where, what, happy,* and *name.*   **M** Play the memory game with your notecards.

N Listen. Look.

SCHOOL ID

Last Name: **Moreno**

First Name: **Maria**

Country: **Mexico**

Address: **2900 W. Manchester Ave. Mesa, Arizona 85209**

Phone: **760-350-1234**

O Underline *M* and *m*.

P Listen. Circle.

1. Where is she from?   a. Mesa, Arizona   b. Mexico

2. Where does she live?   a. Mesa, Arizona   b. Mexico

Q Write.

SCHOOL ID

Last Name: _____

First Name: _____

Country: _____

Address: _____

_____

Phone: _____

Teacher Notes

N Listen and repeat. Track the text.   **O** Underline *M* and *m*.   **P** Listen and circle the answer.

Q Write your information.

5   This Is My Family.   r

A   Listen.   Repeat.   *r*   *r*   *r*   *r*

B   Listen.   Repeat.

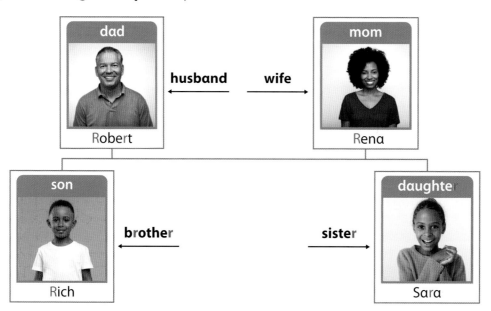

C   Listen.   Circle.

1.   a.   b.   c.

2.   a.   b.   c.

3.   a.   b.   c.

Teacher Notes

A Listen and repeat the *r sound.*   **B** Listen and repeat.   **C** Listen and circle words that begin with *r.*

D Circle.

r	r	v	ו	r	ו	v	r	v
r	v	ו	v	r	r	t	v	r
r	t	r	v	ו	v	ו	v	r

E Write *r*.

F Listen. Repeat. Write *r*.

 1. red ____ose

 2. daughte____

 3. ____ing

 4. fi____st

Teacher Notes

D Circle *r*.　　**E** Write *r*.　　**F** Listen and repeat. Write *r*.

G Write *R*. ✏️

R R R R R R R R R R

R R R R R R R R R R

R

R

H Listen. 👂 **Repeat.** 🗣️ **Write *R*.** ✏️

Robert   **R**ena   **R**ead a book.

_____obert   _____ena   _____ead a book.

I Listen. 👂 **Repeat.** 🗣️

This is my friend, Carina.

this

Nice to meet you, Carina.

J Practice. 🗣️🗣️

Teacher Notes

G Write *R*.   **H** Listen and repeat. Write *R*.   **I** Listen and repeat.   **J** Practice the conversation.

K Listen. Repeat.

A: This is my friend, <u>Robert</u>.

B: I'm happy to meet you, <u>Robert</u>.

L Practice.

M Write *this*.

this

N Listen. Repeat.

A: Spell *this*.
B: *t…h…i…s*

A: Spell *what*.
B: *w…h…a…t*

A: Spell *where*.
B: *w…h…e…r…e*

A: Spell *from*.
B: *f…r…o…m*

A: Spell *happy*.
B: *h…a…p…p…y*

A: Spell *name*.
B: *n…a…m…e*

O Practice.

Teacher Notes

K Listen and repeat. **L** Practice the conversation with your information. **M** Write *this*.
N Spell *this*, *where*, *happy*, *what*, *from*, and *name*. **O** Practice. Play Concentration with *n* words.

P Listen. 🔊 Look. 👁

Redding Family

This is Robert and Rena. They are married. They have one daughter and one son. They are happy.

married

Q Underline *R* and *r*. ✏ Circle *this*. ✏

R Listen. 🔊 Circle. ✏

1. How many daughters do they have? a. one b. two

2. How many sons do they have? a. one b. two

S Write. ✏

> My Family
>
> I am Rena. I have one daughter and one son. I am happy.

T Write. ✏

> My Family
>
> I am single. I have one brother and one sister. I am happy.

single

Teacher Notes

P Listen. Track the words. **Q** Underline *R* and *r*. Circle *this*. **R** Listen. Circle the answer.
S Write. Trace the words. **T** Write. Trace the words.

Put It Together

n, h, wh, w, m, r, a

A Circle.

from

happy

name

where

what

this

```
t  h  i  s  e  v  t  w  h  a  t  l  i  k  d  a
h  g  m  m  d  e  k  a  p  h  s  z  a  v  o  o
a  t  c  z  y  p  u  z  t  n  a  m  e  g  q  b
a  p  e  s  l  s  e  f  j  f  i  c  q  j  m  i
f  r  o  m  y  d  s  l  j  i  b  d  k  b  z  m
z  w  h  e  r  e  p  d  h  a  p  p  y  s  p  f
m  o  u  d  t  w  i  l  f  k  h  n  z  z  n  v
u  b  l  h  k  w  r  i  t  e  t  b  z  x  s  i
w  n  t  v  f  s  g  h  b  z  e  a  k  l  s  n
k  o  m  c  s  k  v  q  d  z  c  i  r  c  l  e
s  z  e  c  t  u  q  d  m  x  t  a  e  j  u  v
r  e  a  d  m  l  r  p  m  x  c  l  t  c  t  j
```

B Write a.

a a a a a a a a a a a a

a a a a a a a a a a a a

a

a

Teacher Notes

A Find and circle the words.   B Write a.

C Listen. Repeat.

1. hat

2. mat

3. rat

4. cat

D Listen. Repeat. Write *a*.

1. m___a___p

2. h_____ppy

237 W. Broadway
Anaheim, CA 92801

3. _____ddress

NAME CARD
Last Name: **Mendoza**

4. l_____st name

E Write *A*.

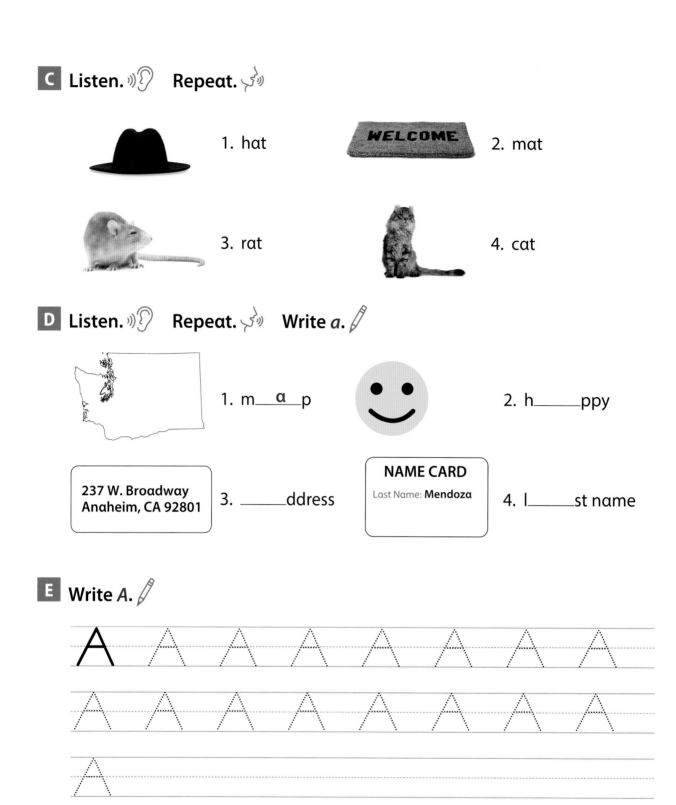

Teacher Notes

C Listen and repeat.   **D** Listen and repeat. Write *a*.   **E** Write *A*.

F Practice.

What's your first name?
Maria

What's your last name?
Mendoza

Where are you from?
Mexico

Where do you live?
Mesa, Arizona

G Write *live*, *first*, **and** *last*.

live

first

last

H Listen. Spell.

Spell *live*.	Spell *first*.	Spell *last*.
Spell *this*.	Spell *from*.	Spell *where*.
Spell *what*.	Spell *happy*.	Spell *name*.

Teacher Notes

F Practice. Ask two classmates the questions. Ask them to spell. Write their answers.

G Write *live*, *first*, and *last*.   H Listen. Spell. Play running dictation.

I Listen. 🦻 Look. 👁

Nasham Haj is from Syria. She lives in Miami, Florida. She is married. She has one daughter and three sons.

J Circle *from*, *lives*, *married*, *daughter*, **and** *sons*. ✏️

K Listen. 🦻 Circle. ✏️

1. What is her first name?   a. Nasham   b. Haj

2. Where is she from?   a. Miami   b. Syria

L Write. ✏️

My name is Nasham Haj. I am from
Syria. I live in Miami, Florida. I am married.

M Write. ✏️

My name is _____. I am
from _____. I live in _____,
_____. I am _____.

Teacher Notes

I Listen and track the words.   **J** Circle *from*, *lives*, *married*, *daughter*, and *sons*.

K Listen and circle the answer.   **L** Trace the text.   **M** Write your information.

52 fifty-two

Quiz

A Listen. Circle.

n 1. a. 　b. 　c.

w 2. a. 　b. 　c.

h 3. a. 　b. 　c.

m 4. a. 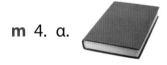　b. 　c.

r 5. a. 　b. 　c.

B Listen. Write.

1. What is your first name?

2. What is your last name?

3. Where do you live?

4. Where are you from?

Teacher Notes

A Listen and circle the word that has the letter sound you see in red at the beginning.

B Listen to the questions. Write answers with your information.

2 The Classroom

Teacher Notes

Point to the door. What is the room number?

Find the calendar. Point to the year. Point to the number words.

1 My Friend *f, fr, fl*

A **Listen.** **Repeat.**

f *f* *f* *f* *fr* *fr* *fr* *fr* *fl* *fl* *fl* *fl*

B **Listen. Repeat.**

Flag of Haiti

Flag of France

Profile
First Name: Fabiola
Last Name: Jean
Language: French

Profile
First Name: Franc
Last Name: Lane
Language: French

C **Listen. Circle.**

1. a. b. c.

2. a. b. c.

3. a. b. c.

Teacher Notes

A Listen and repeat the letter sounds. **B** Listen and repeat. **C** Listen and circle words that have the *f* sound.

D Circle the letter *f*.

f	(f)	ʄ	ʄ	f	f	ʄ	f	ʄ
f	s	S	f	t	f	f	t	s
f	t	f	ʄ	f	s	t	f	f

E Write *f*.

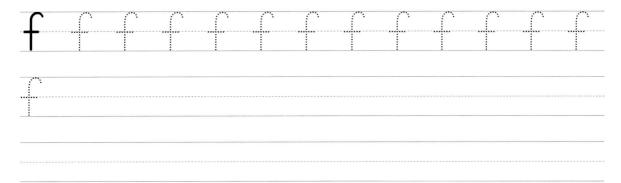

F Listen and repeat. Write *f*.

1. __f__oot

2. _____ork

3. _____lower

4. _____ly

5. _____ive

6. _____rog

G Write *F.* 🖊

F F F F F F F F F

F

H Listen and repeat. Write *F* and *f.*

1. Fabiola is from Haiti.

    _____ abiola is from Haiti.

2. Franc is from France.

    _____ ranc is from _____ rance.

3. My first name is Fred.

    My _____ name is _____ .

Teacher Notes

G Write *F.*   **H** Listen and repeat. Write *F* and *f.* Point out to students that there is a mix of uppercase and lowercase when you get to the third item.

58 fifty-eight

I **Listen and repeat.**

A: This is my friend Fay.
   She is from Canada.

B: Nice to meet you, Fay.

friend

J **Practice.**

K **Listen and repeat.**

A: Hi Bo, this is my friend Fay. She is from Canada.

B: Hi, Fay. It's nice to meet you. I'm from China.

L **Practice.**

M **Write** *friend*.

friend friend

N **Listen and repeat.**

A: Spell *friend*.

B: f...r...i...e...n...d

Teacher Notes

I Listen and repeat.   **J** Practice the conversation with your information.   **K** Listen and repeat.

L Practice the conversation with your information.   **M** Write *friend*.   **N** Listen and repeat.

O Listen. 🔊 Look. 👁

Fabiola

This is Fabiola. She is my friend. She is from Haiti. She speaks French and Creole.

P Underline the *F*, *Fr*, and *fr*. ___✏️   Circle *friend*. ✏️

Q Listen and circle.

1. What is her name?   a. Fabiola   b. Haiti

2. Where is she from?   a. Fabiola   b. Haiti

R Write. ✏️

This is my friend Franc. He is
from France. He speaks French.

S Write.

This is my friend _____ .

He is from _____ .

He speaks _____ .

Teacher Notes

O Listen. Track the words.   **P** Underline the *F*, *Fr*, and *fr*. Circle *friend*.   **Q** Listen and circle the answer.

R Write. Trace the words.   **S** Write about a friend in the class. Then introduce your friend to a partner.

A Listen and repeat.

p p p p

B Listen and repeat.

| pencil | ruler | pen |

paper

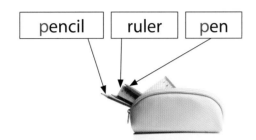
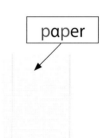

C Listen and repeat. Circle.

1. a.  (b.)   c.

2. a.   b.   c.

3. a.   b.   c.

4. a.  b.   c.

Teacher Notes

A Listen and repeat the letter sound.   **B** Listen and repeat.

C Listen and repeat. Circle words that have the *p* sound.

D Circle *p*.

p	b	(p)	d	p	q	q	b	b
p	p	b	d	d	q	q	b	p
p	q	p	9	e	p	p	d	p

E Write *p*.

p P P P P P P P P P P P

p

F Listen and repeat. Write *p*.

1. __p__alm tree

2. _____aper

3. _____ot

4. _____lane

Teacher Notes

D Circle *p*. **E** Write *p*. **F** Listen and repeat. Write *p*.

62 sixty-two

G Write *P*.

P P P P P P P P P P

P

H Listen and repeat. Write *P*.

Please, take out a pencil.

_____lease, take out a pencil.

Please, open your book.

_____lease, open your book.

I Listen and repeat. Practice.

A: Hello, class.

B: Hello!

A: Please, take out a pencil and paper.

Teacher Notes

G Write *P*.　**H** Listen and repeat. Write *P*.　**I** Listen and repeat. Practice. Have students practice in pairs.

J Listen and repeat. 🔊👂🗣️

Please, take out a <u>pencil</u>.

please

K Practice with *a pen*, *your books*, and *a ruler*. 🗣️

L Write *Please*. ✏️

Please

M Spell. 🔤

A: Spell *please*.

B: *p…l…e…a…s…e*

A: Spell *friend*.

B: *f…r…i…e…n…d*

N Practice. 🗣️

Teacher Notes

J Listen and repeat.　　**K** Practice with *a pen, your books*, and *a ruler*.

L Write *Please*.　　**M** Spell.　　**N** Practice spelling the words with alphabet cards.

O **Listen. Look.** 👁

Classroom Instructions

1. Please sit down.
2. Please take out a pen and paper.
3. Please write your name.
4. Please open your books.
5. Please listen carefully.

P **Underline** *P* **and** *p*. ✏ **Circle** *Please*. ✏

Q **Listen and circle.**

1. What do students write?   a. their names   b. their books

2. What do students open?   a. their names   b. their books

R **Practice.**

A: Please sit down.
   Please take out a pen and paper.

B: Please open your books.
   Please listen carefully.

S **Write.**

Please sit down.
Please take out a pen and paper.
Please open your books.
Please listen carefully.

Teacher Notes

O Listen. Track the words.   **P** Underline *P* and *p*. Circle *Please*.   **Q** Listen and circle the answer.
R Practice following the commands with your partner.   **S** Write.

3 My Classroom   c, ck

A Listen and repeat. c c c c ck ck ck ck

B Listen and repeat.

bookcase   **wall clock**   **cabinet**   **trashcan**   computer

C Listen. Circle.

1. a.   (b.)   c.

2. a.   b.   c.

3. a.   b.    c.

D Circle c.

c	(c)	c	⊃	⊃	c	c	0	c
c	u	⊏	c	c	⊃	c	u	c
c	c	c	c	⊃	⊃	c	u	⊏

E Write c. ✎

C c c c c c c c c c c c c c C

c

F Listen and repeat. Write c.

1. __c__rayons

2. _____ar

3. _____ap

4. _____abinet

G Write C.

C C C C C C C C C C

C

H Listen and repeat. Write C.

Carolina is a student.

_____ arolina is a student.

Carolina is in the classroom.

_____ arolina is in the classroom.

I Listen and repeat.

A: Excuse me. Where's the clock?

B: It's over there on the wall.

J Practice.

Teacher Notes

G Write C.   H Listen and repeat. Write C.   I Listen and repeat.   J Practice the conversation in I.

68 sixty-eight

K Listen and repeat.

A: Where's the clock?
B: It's on the wall.

A: Where's the student?
B: She's in the classroom.

L Practice.

M Write *in* and *on*.

in   in

on   on

N Spell.

A: Spell *in*.
B: i...n

A: Spell *please*.
B: p...l...e...a...s...e

A: Spell *on*.
B: o...n

A: Spell *friend*.
B: f...r...i...e...n...d

O Practice.

Teacher Notes

K Listen and repeat.   L Practice the conversation.   M Write *in* and *on*.   N Spell.
O Practice spelling the words with letter cards.

sixty-nine   **69**

P Listen. Look.

My name is Carol. I'm in my classroom in South Carolina. There are desks, a computer, and a cabinet in the classroom. The computer is on a table in the back.

Q Underline *C* and *c*. Circle *in*.

R Listen and circle.

1. Where is Carol?   a. in the classroom   b. on the classroom

2. What is on a table?   a. a book   b. a computer

S Write.

My name is Edgar. I'm in my classroom. There are desks, a bookcase, and a cabinet in the classroom.

T Write.

My name is _____. I'm in my _____. There are desks and _____ in the classroom.

Teacher Notes

P Listen. Track the words.   **Q** Underline *C* and *c*. Circle *in*.   **R** Listen and circle the correct answer.
S Write. Trace the words.   **T** Write about things in your classroom.

70   seventy

4 It's at 3:00. s

A Listen and repeat. s s s s

B Listen and repeat.

	Saturday	Sunday
5:00 PM (five o'clock)	5:47 ☀	
6:00 PM (six o'clock)	dinner 🍴	dinner 🍴
7:00 PM (seven o'clock)	movie 🎬	soccer game ⚽

C Listen. Circle. ✏

1. a.   (b.)   c.

2. a.   b.   c.

3. a.   b.   c.

4. a.   b.   c.

Teacher Notes

A Listen and repeat the letter sound.   **B** Listen and repeat.   **C** Listen. Circle the words that have the *s* sound.

D Circle s.

s	ⓢ	3	s	ƨ	s	ƨ	s	c
s	c	c	s	c	ƨ	s	s	ƨ
s	f	s	ƨ	c	y	s	ƨ	s

E Write s.

S   s   s   s   s   s   s   s   s   s   s   s   s

s

F Listen and repeat. Write s.

1. __s__andwich

2. ____ix

3. ____ock

4. ____lide

Teacher Notes

D Circle s.　　**E** Write s.　　**F** Listen and repeat. Write s.

72　seventy-two

G Write *S*.

S S S S S S S S S S

S

H Listen and repeat. Write *S*.

SUNDAY
SUN

Sunday is a good day.

_____ unday is a good day.

Sam eats at 5:00.

_____ am eats at 5:00.

I Listen and repeat. Practice.

What time is dinner?

It's at 6:00.

Teacher Notes

G Write *S*.   **H** Listen and repeat. Write *S*.   **I** Listen and repeat. Practice the conversation.

J **Listen and repeat.**

	Saturday	Sunday
5:00 PM (five o'clock)	5:47 ☀	
6:00 PM (six o'clock)	dinner 🍽	dinner 🍽
7:00 PM (seven o'clock)	movie 🍿	soccer game ⚽

A: What time is the <u>soccer game</u>?

B: It's at 7:00.

at

K **Practice with** *the soccer game*, *sunset*, **and** *the movie.*

L **Write** *at.*

at   at

M **Spell.** ABC

at   in   on   please   friend

N **Practice.**

Teacher Notes

J Listen and repeat.   **K** Practice with *the soccer game*, *sunset*, and *the movie*.   **L** Write *at*.
M Spell the words.   **N** Practice spelling words from the lesson.

O Listen. Look. 👁

Schedule

sunset

	Saturday	Sunday
5:00 PM (five o'clock)	movie 🍿	dinner 🍽
6:00 PM (six o'clock)	6:30 🌅	
7:00 PM (seven o'clock)	dinner 🍽	TV 📺

P Underline *S* and *s*. ✏

Q Listen and circle. ✏

1. What time is dinner on Sunday?   a. 5:00   b. 7:00

2. What time is dinner on Saturday?   a. 5:00   b. 7:00

R Write.

5:00		
6:00		

S Practice.

Teacher Notes

O Listen. Track the words.   **P** Underline *S* and *s*.   **Q** Listen and circle the answers.

R Write your schedule.   **S** Practice. Ask and answer questions about when you eat dinner. Stand under the

time.

What's Today? d

A Listen and repeat. 🔊 d d d d

B Listen and repeat.

JANUARY						
Monday	Tuesday	Wednesday	Thursday	Friday	Saturday	Sunday
31	1	*Today* 2	3	4	5	6
	New Year's Day		First Day of School	School	Dad's Birthday	

C Listen. Circle.

1. (a.)   b.   c.

2. a.    b.   c.

3. a.    b.   c.

4. a.    b.   c.

Teacher Notes

A Listen and repeat the letter sound.   **B** Listen and repeat.   **C** Listen. Circle the words with the *d* sound.

D Circle d.

d	d	b	b	b	d	d	b	d
d	b	d	p	p	q	d	d	q
d	6	b	d	ə	b	d	b	d

E Write d.

F Listen and repeat. Write d.

  1. __d__ ay

  2. _____ish

 3. _____og

  4. _____octor

Teacher Notes

D Circle d.　　E Write d.　　F Listen and repeat. Write d.

G Write *D.* ✏️

H Listen and repeat. 🔊👂 Write *D.*

New Year's Day   Dad's birthday is today.

New Year's _____ay.   _____ad's birthday is today.

I Listen and repeat. Practice. 🗣️🗣️

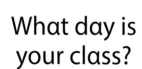

What day is your class?

It's on Tuesday, Wednesday, and Thursday.

Teacher Notes

G Write *D.*   **H** Listen and repeat. Write *D.*   **I** Listen and repeat. Practice.

J Listen and repeat. Practice.

A: When is your class?

B: My class? It's <u>today at 10:00 am</u>.

my	your

K Write *my* and *your*.

my

your

L Spell.

| my | your | at | in | on | please | friend |

M Practice.

Teacher Notes

J Listen and repeat. Practice.   K Write *my* and *your*.   L Spell the words.

M Practice. Play concentration with words from **L**.

N Listen. Look. 🔊👂 👁

MARCH						
Monday	**Tuesday**	**Wednesday**	**Thursday**	**Friday**	**Saturday**	**Sunday**
2	3	4 Debra's birthday	5	6 Daria's birthday	7	8
9 school day	10 school day	11 school day	12 school day	13 school day	14	15

O Underline *D* and *d*.

P Listen and circle. 🖊

1. What day is Daria's birthday?   a. Wednesday   b. Friday

2. What day is Debra's birthday?   a. Wednesday   b. Friday

Q Write. ✏

_____		
Monday	**Tuesday**	**Wednesday**

Teacher Notes

N Listen. Track the words.   **O** Underline *D* and *d*.   **P** Listen and circle the answers.

Q Write events in your calendar.

80   eighty

6

Put It Together

f, fr, fl, p, c, ck, s, d

A Circle.

friend	w v k k e j e l g t p z m p x e
	h a l n t f r b o j y s v l p g
please	i h p q k e v k m a g l m e a y
	t m y n e r b u j d c j o a e i
your	d k h c e x z h p t z e t s q e
my	h b v y i a m a c o a s j e z s
	h m v o k e l y z z m o a b z z
at	i n a u f r i e n d o i a z d d
on	c a x r s l d i r n n z y d q d
	b w b g e t z b n w x i c f r b
in	t y e m o k x a f a s z r e m m
	j b o h z d g m i t o p l a s b

a = α

B Write *a*.

α α α α α α α α α α α α α

α

Teacher Notes

A Find and circle the words.

B Write *a*. Remind students there are two lower case a's: one we write with a pencil and one we type.

C Listen and repeat. 🔊

 1. day

 2. say

 3. cake

 4. snake

D Listen and repeat. Write *a*. ✏️

 1. p____y

 2. pl____y

 3. b____ke

 4. n____me

E Write *A*.

Teacher Notes

C Listen and repeat.   D Listen and repeat. Write *a*.   E Write *A*.

F Practice. 👂 👂 Write.

What's your name?	Where are you from?
Omar	Saudi Arabia

When is dinner?	What days do you go to school?
5:00 PM	Monday, Tuesday, Wednesday

G Write *go*, *school*, **and** *you*.

go go

school school

you you

H Spell.

Spell *go*.   Spell *school*.   Spell *you*.   Spell *my*.

Spell *your*.   Spell *at*.   Spell *in*.   Spell *on*.

Spell *please*.   Spell *friend*.

Teacher Notes

F Practice. Ask and answer the questions with your classmates. Write their answers.

G Write *go*, *school*, and *you*.   **H** Play running dictation in groups.

I Listen. Look.

Omar is from Saudi Arabia. He goes to school on Monday, Tuesday, and Wednesday at 6:00 PM. He eats dinner at 5:00 PM.

J Circle *from*, *goes*, *Monday*, *Tuesday*, and *Wednesday*.

K Listen. Circle.

1. What time is school? a. 5:00 PM b. 6:00 PM
2. What time is dinner? a. 5:00 PM b. 6:00 PM

L Write.

My name is Omar. I'm in my classroom. There are books, desks, and a computer in my classroom.

M Write.

My name is _____. I'm in _____. There are _____, _____, and a _____ in the classroom.

Teacher Notes

I Listen. Track the words. **J** Circle *from*, *goes*, *Monday*, *Tuesday*, and *Wednesday*.

K Listen. Circle the answers. **L** Write. Trace the words. **M** Write your information.

84 eighty-four

Quiz

f 1. a. b. c.

p 2. a.  b. c.

c 3. a. b. c.

s 4. a.  b. c.

d 5. a. b. c.

B Listen. Write.

1. What time is your class?

2. What days do you have class?

3. Where are you from?

Teacher Notes

A Listen and circle words that begin with the letter sound you see in red at the beginning.

B Listen. Write your information.

3 Food

Look. Point to the sale. Point to the price. Point to the open cashier.

1 Let's Shop b

A Listen and repeat. *b* *b* *b* *b*

B Listen and repeat.

Family Market

bananas	beans	butter
$1	$1	$3

C Listen and repeat. Check.

✓ 1.   ☐ 2.   ☐ 3.

☐ 4.   ☐ 5.   ☐ 6.

☐ 7.   ☐ 8.   ☐ 9.

D Circle *b*.

b	ⓑ	d	d	b	d	d	b	d
b	d	b	6	d	6	b	p	b
b	6	d	p	b	6	b	6	b

E **Write** *b.*

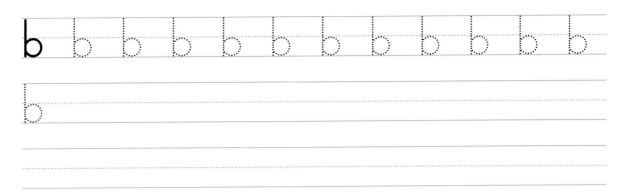

F **Listen and repeat. Write** *b.*

 1. __b__ ananas

 2. _____eans

 3. _____utter

 4. _____ag

 5. _____read

 6. _____asket

G **Write** *B.*

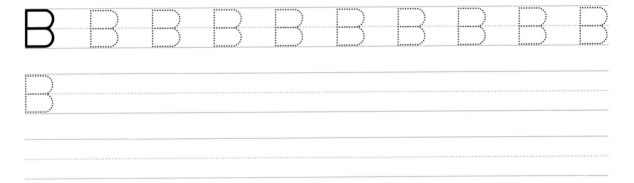

H **Listen and repeat. Write** *B.*

1. **B**ananas are $1.

_____ananas are $1.

2. **B**eans are $1.

_____eans are $1.

3. **B**utter is $3.

_____utter is $3.

I Listen and repeat.

A: <u>Bananas</u>! How much?

B: <u>$1</u>.

J Practice with *beans* and *butter*.

K Listen and repeat.

A: I buy <u>bananas</u> every week.

B: I like <u>bananas</u> too.

buy	like

L Practice with *beans*, *butter*, and *bread*.

beans   butter   bread

M Write *buy* and *like*.

buy

like

N Spell.

A: Spell *buy*.

B: *b…u…y*

A: Spell *like*.

B: *l…i…k…e*

O **Listen. Look.**

Beto buys bananas, buns, and butter. He likes vegetables too. He likes beans.

> buy – buys
> like – likes

fruits and vegetables

P **Underline *B* and *b*. Circle *buys* and *likes*.**

Q **Listen and circle.**

1. Who buys butter?
   a. Beto buys butter.
   b. You buy butter.

2. What vegetable does he like?
   a. bananas.
   b. beans.

R **Listen. Write.**

I buy bananas and bread.

I like vegetables too.

I like broccoli, beans, and bell peppers.

broccoli

bell peppers

S **Write.**

1. I _____ bananas and bread.

2. I _____ vegetables too.

3. I _____ broccoli, beans, and bell peppers.

2 Make a List   *ch*

A **Listen and repeat.**   *ch*   *ch*   *ch*   *ch*

B **Listen and repeat.**

sandwich
ketchup
chicken
chips
cheese

C **Listen. Check.**

✓ 1.   □ 2.   □ 3.

□ 4.   □ 5.   □ 6.

□ 7.   □ 8.   □ 9.

D **Circle *ch*.**

ch	c	ck	(ch)	sh	c	ch	cl	ch
ch	ch	c	sh	sh	ch	h	ck	c
ch	ch	sh	sk	ch	h	hc	ch	cl

E Write *ch*.

ch   ch   ch   ch   ch   ch   ch   ch   ch

ch

F Listen and repeat. Write *ch*.

  1. __ch__ air

 2. _____ili pepper

  3. _____eesecake

  4. ket_____up

  5. pea_____

  6. kit_____en

G Write *Ch*.

Ch   Ch   Ch   Ch   Ch   Ch   Ch   Ch

Ch

H Listen and repeat. Write *Ch*.

1. **Ch**uck likes chicken.

_____uck likes chicken.

2. **Ch**ili peppers are spicy.

_____ili peppers are spicy.

I **Listen and repeat.**

> What do we need at the store?

> Cheese.

need

J **Practice with *chicken*, *chips*, and *cheesecake*.**

K **Listen and repeat.**

A: What do we need at the store?

B: Cheese, chicken, and chips.

cheese	chips
cherries	chocolate
chicken	ketchup
chili peppers	peaches

L **Practice.**

M **Write *need*.**

need

N **Spell.**

A: Spell *buy*.

B: *b…u…y*

A: Spell *like*.

B: *l…i…k…e*

A: Spell *need*.

B: *n…e…e…d*

O **Practice with your alphabet cards.**

P Listen. Look.

Omar's Shopping List

cheese	bread
bananas	spinach
green beans	peaches
chicken	

Q Underline *ch*.

R Listen and circle.

1. Omar needs cheese.   a. yes   b. no
2. Omar needs chili peppers.   a. yes   b. no

S Listen. Write.

Omar's Shopping List

cheese   bread

bananas   spinach

green beans   peaches

chicken

Can I Help You? s

A Listen and repeat. s   s   s   s

B Listen and repeat.

Lennie's Café

Sandwiches
Grilled cheese
sandwich $7
Tuna sandwich $7

**Soups
and Salads**
Vegetable soup $4
Green salad $4

Side Orders
French fries $3
Fruit $3

Drinks
Soda $2
Tea $2

C Listen and repeat. Check.

✓ 1.   ☐ 2.   ☐ 3.

☐ 4.   ☐ 5.   ☐ 6.

☐ 7.   ☐ 8.   ☐ 9.

D Circle s.

s	f	(s)	z	z	s	s	z	s
s	z	s	s	s	z	z	s	z
s	s	z	z	s	z	s	s	s

E Write **s**.

S s s s s s s s s s s s s

s

F Listen and write **s**.

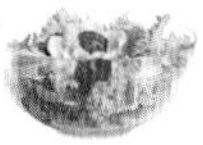

1. _s_ alad    2. ___oup    3. ___oda

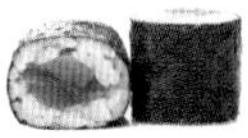

4. ___ushi    5. ___ trawberries 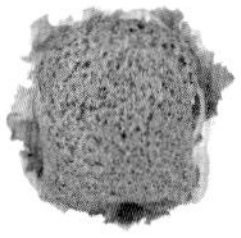   6. ___ andwich

G Write **S**.

S S S S S S S S S S S

S

H Listen, repeat, and write **S**.

Susan likes sandwiches.   Salads are healthy.

_____usan likes sandwiches.   _____alads are healthy.

I Listen and repeat.

Can I help you?

server   customer (guest)

J Listen and repeat.

(and)

Server: Can I help you?

Customer: Yes, one <u>tuna sandwich</u> and one <u>soda</u>, please.

Server: <u>One tuna sandwich</u> and <u>a soda</u>, great!

Customer: Thank you.

K Practice with *grilled cheese sandwich*, *french fries*, *soup*, *salad*, and *tea*.

Lennie's Café

Sandwiches
Grilled cheese
sandwich $7
Tuna sandwich $7

**Soups
and Salads**
Vegetable soup $4
Green salad $4

Side Orders
French fries $3
Fruit $3

Drinks
Soda $2
Tea $2

L Write *and*.

and

M Spell.

A: Spell *buy*.

B: b...u...y

A: Spell *like*.

B: l...i...k...e

A: Spell *need*.

B: n...e...e...d

A: Spell *and*.

B: a...n...d

N Read. Underline *S* and *s*.

Lennie's Café
3298 W. Manchester Ave.
Kansas City, MS

SALE
02/21/2024   10:58 AM

2 grilled cheese sandwiches	$ 7.00
2 french fries	$ 3.00
2 teas	$ 2.00
2 green salads	$ 4.00

SUBTOTAL: $16.00
TAX: $1.42
TOTAL: $17.42

TIP: _____
TOTAL: _____

O Listen and circle.

1. What is the name of the restaurant?

   a. Manchester Ave.   b. Lennie's Café   c. $17.42

2. What's the total?

   a. $16.00   b. $1.42   c. $17.42

P Listen.

Lennie's Café

Qty	Item	
1	tuna sandwich	$ 7.00
1	fruit	$ 3.00
1	tea	$ 2.00

Q Write.

Lennie's Café

Qty	Item	
1	tuna _____	$ _____
1	fruit	$ _____
1	tea	$ _____

4 Ketchup, Please k

A Listen and repeat. *k k k k*

B Listen and repeat *k*.

Chicken Kabobs

Ingredients:

chicken

onions

green peppers

Teriyaki sauce

C Listen. Check.

✓ 1.		☐ 2.		☐ 3. 	
☐ 4.		☐ 5. 		☐ 6.	
☐ 7.		☐ 8. 		☐ 9.	

D Circle *k*.

k	ⓚ	k	k	b	q	k	q	L
k	q	k	L	k	L	b	k	k
k	k	b	k	L	k	b	k	q

E Write *k*.

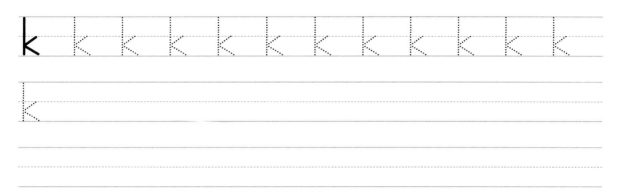

F Listen and repeat. Write *k*.

 1. __k__ite

 2. _____iwi

 3. _____itchen

 4. _____eys

 5. cloc _____

 6. des_____

G Write *K*.

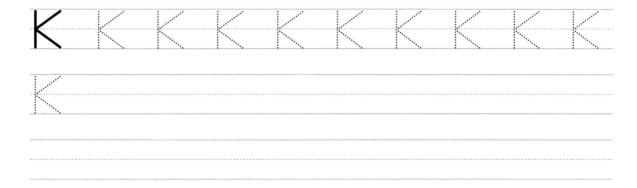

H Listen and repeat. Write *K*.

1. **K**evin is a student.

2. **K**abobs are delicious.

_____ evin is a student.

_____ abobs are delicious.

I Listen and repeat.

A: Do you want <u>mustard</u>?

B: No thank you. I want <u>ketchup</u>.

hot dog

cheese

pickles

ketchup

mustard

chili

J Practice with *pickles*, *cheese*, **and** *chili*.

want

K Listen and repeat. Practice.

A: What do you want on it?

B: I want chili and pickles, please.

L Write *want*.

want

M Spell.

| want | and | need | like | buy |

N Practice.

n e e d

O Listen. Track the words.

Chicken Kabobs

#1 STEP 1
- CUT CHICKEN
- CUT ONIONS
- CUT PEPPERS

#2 STEP 2
- PUT ON SKEWERS

#3 STEP 3
- ADD TERIYAKI SAUCE
- COOK KABOBS

P Underline *K* and *k*.

Q Listen and circle.

1. When do you cook?   a. Step #1   b. Step #2   c. Step #3
2. When do you cut?   a. Step #1   b. Step #2   c. Step #3

R Listen. Track the words.

I want a hamburger. I like pickles and cheese on my hamburger. I want ketchup, lettuce, and tomatoes.

hamburger

S Write.

I _____ a hamburger.

I _____ pickles and cheese on my hamburger.

I _____ ketchup, lettuce, and tomatoes.

What's for Lunch?   l

A Listen and repeat. /   /   /   /

B Listen and repeat.

Meal Plan

	Monday, April 23	Tuesday, April 24
Breakfast	Cheese Omelet	Cereal and Fruit
Lunch	Chicken Salad	Chili
Dinner	Lasagna	Chicken Noodle Soup

C Listen and repeat. Check.

☑ 1.   ☐ 2.   ☐ 3.

☐ 4.   ☐ 5.   ☐ 6.

D Circle *L* and *l*.

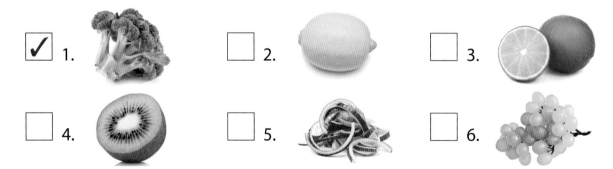

l	ⓛ	t	l	l	1	l	1	T
L	⅃	L	⅃	1	L	T	L	⊥
L	L	⅃	L	T	⊥	⅃	1	L

E Write *l*.

F Listen and repeat. Write *l*.

1. ___l__obster   2. be___ ___ pepper   3. me_____on

4. _____emon   5. _____imes   6. meat_____oaf

G Write *L*.

H Listen and repeat. Write *L* and *l*.

1. **L**eticia **l**ikes soup.   2. **L**unch is my favorite mea**l**.

   _____eticia _____ikes soup.   _____unch is my favorite mea_____.

I Listen and repeat.

salad

chili

lasagna

soup

A: What's *for* lunch?

B: <u>Salad!</u>

> for   eat

J Practice with *chili*, *lasagna*, and *soup*.

K Practice.

A: What do you *eat for* dinner?

B: _____

L Write *for* and *eat*.

for

eat

M Spell.

> eat   for   want   and   need   like   buy

N Practice with words from **M.**

Meal Plan

	Wedneday, April 25	Thursday, April 26
Breakfast	Eggs and Melon	Omelet
Lunch	Chicken Noodle Soup	Tuna Sandwich
Dinner	Meatloaf	Chili

P Underline *L* and *l*.

Q Listen and circle.

1. What meal is for dinner?   a. chili   b. omelet

2. What meal is for lunch?   a. tuna sandwich   b. eggs and melon

R Write and talk.

Meal Plan

	Wednesday, April 25	Thursday, April 26
Breakfast	eggs and _____	_____
Lunch	chicken noodle soup	tuna sandwich
Dinner	_____	_____

6 Put It Together   b, ch, s, k, l, e, ea, ee

A Circle.

buy ~~buy~~

like

need

and

want

for

eat

```
m h j u b u t x m w a n t q i h
q l b k k n o l u l u m h v e a
i g c v v e t f v b o x s q w n
m h u n i e e o h s u t n u m t
e i e l p d i t a v q r m e v
c t u n e u c e z l w i u n k f
u r e i a w g s f x n z p i p o
r i j e o x i q f l y g u p w r
e z b f e (b u y) u a n d e a t m
d f g m w y f i l q t d w h n l
p j q n p t n l i k e h l n h f
r y r t y j o s w o s o d s j g
```

B Write the words.

buy

like

need

and

want

for

eat

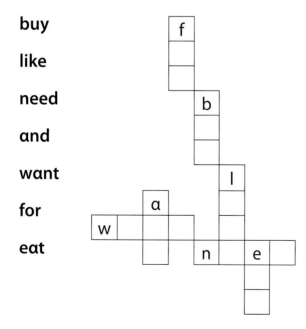

C Write *e* and *ea*.

e e e e e e e e e e e e

e

ea ea ea ea ea ea ea ea

ea

D Listen and repeat.

 1. cheese

 2. meat

 3. me

 4. eat

E Listen and repeat. Write *e*, *ea*, or *ee*.

 1. f__ee__t

 2. t_____

 3. P_____te

 4. _____r

F Practice.

What do you like for breakfast?	What do you eat for dinner?
What do you want for lunch?	

G Write *meal*, *cook* and *cut*.

meal

cook

cut

H Play. Spell.

Spell buy.

b...u...y.

go	school
your	at
buy	like
for	eat
you	my
in	on
need	and
please	friend
want	

I Play. Think of words that have the letters *b*, *ch*, *k*, *l*, and *s*.

J Listen and look.

Lucy likes fruit salad. She needs apples, peaches, watermelon, and strawberries. She buys fruit every day.

K Circle *and*, *needs*, *buys*, and *likes*.

L Listen and circle.

1. What does she like? a. soup b. fruit salad

2. What does she buy every day? a. fruit b. salad

M Listen and write.

I like vegetable soup. I need beans, onions, carrots, and potatoes. I buy vegetables every day.

N Write.

I _____ vegetable soup. I _____ beans, onions, carrots, and potatoes. I _____ vegetables every day.

Quiz

b 1. a. (b.)  c.

ch 2. a.  b. c.

s 3. a.  b.  c.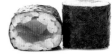

k 4. a. b. c.

l 5. a. b.  c.

B Listen. Write.

 1. ___ ___ili

 2. ___anana

 3. ___ettuce

4. ___andwich

5. ___abob

C **Listen. Write.**

1. Breakfast, _____ unch, and dinner.

2. We need _____read for sandwiches.

3. She wants bananas, strawberries, _____ oranges.

D **Write six words you know.**

1. _____

_____

2. _____

_____

3. _____

_____

4. _____

_____

5. _____

_____

6. _____

_____

4 Shopping

MEN'S CLOTHING

WOMEN'S CLOTHING

CHILDREN'S CLOTHING

FITTING ROOM

HOMEWARE

RESTROOMS

DISCOUNT

ESCALATORS

ELEVATORS

RETURNS

CASHIER

Look. Choose three signs. What do the signs mean?

1 What to Wear sh

A **Listen and repeat.** *sh* *sh* *sh* *sh*

B **Listen and repeat.**

Shop

shorts

shoes

T-**sh**irts

shirt

C **Listen and repeat. Check *sh*.**

✓ 1.   ☐ 2.   ☐ 3.

☐ 4.   ☐ 5.   ☐ 6.

☐ 7.   ☐ 8.   ☐ 9.

D **Circle *sh*.**

sh	(sh)	hs	ch	sh	5h	s	sq	sh
sh	ch	c	sh	sh	ch	hs	ck	c

E Write *sh*.

sh ‥sh‥ ‥sh‥ ‥sh‥ ‥sh‥ ‥sh‥ ‥sh‥ ‥sh‥ ‥sh‥

sh

F Listen and repeat. Write *sh*.

1. __sh__orts    2. di_____   3. _____ip

4. ca_____   5. _____rimp   6. _____irt

G Write *Sh*.

Sh ‥Sh‥ ‥Sh‥ ‥Sh‥ ‥Sh‥ ‥Sh‥ ‥Sh‥ ‥Sh‥ ‥Sh‥

Sh

H Listen and repeat. Write *Sh* and *sh*.

1. **Sh**erry wears T-shirts.   2. **Sh**oes are for the feet.

   _____erry wears T-_____irts.   _____oes are for the feet.

I Listen and repeat.

I like your shirt.

Thanks. I like it too!

too

J Practice with *shoes, pants, dress,* and *shorts*.

K Listen and repeat.

PANTS

DRESS

SHORTS

SHOES

A: I like your shirt.

B: I do too. It's my favorite.

L Practice the conversation.

M Write *too*.

too

N Spell.

A: Spell *too*.

B: *t…o…o*

O Listen. Track the words.

LAKE SHASTA TRIP

- 1 shirt
- 2 pairs of pants
- 1 pair of shoes
- 1 pair of shorts

P Underline *Sh* and *sh*.

Q Listen and circle.

1. Shawn needs 1 pair of shorts. a. true b. false
2. Shawn needs 2 shirts. a. true b. false

R Listen and write the *sh* words.

Kerry packs to see Aunt Shelby. He needs three shirts, two pairs of shoes, two pairs of pants, and one pair of shorts.

Trip to see Aunt _____

3 _____

2 pairs of _____

2 pairs of pants

1 pair of _____ _____

1 = 1

2 It's Yellow! *y, bl*

A **Listen and repeat.**   y   y   y   y   *bl*   *bl*   *bl*   *bl*

B **Listen and repeat.**

Yuma Park

blue

yoga

black

yellow

C **Listen and repeat. Circle words with *y* and *bl*.**

1.   2.   3.

4.   5.   6.

7.   8.   9.

D **Circle *y*.**

y	ⓨ	v	g	v	g	ʎ	v	y
y	g	v	y	g	ʎ	y	g	ʎ

E Write y.

y y y y y y y y y y y y y

y

F Listen and repeat. Write y.

1. _y_ogurt   2. ___arn   3. ___ellow

4. ___oung   5. ___es   6. ___oga

G Write Y.

Y Y Y Y Y Y Y Y Y Y

Y

H Listen and repeat. Write Y.

1. I want to go to **Y**uma Park.

   I want to go to ___uma Park.

2. **Y**ellow is my favorite color.

   ___ellow is my favorite color.

I **Listen and repeat.**

A: What color is the shirt?

B: It's red.

red   blue   black

J **Practice with *blue, black, yellow, green,* and *orange.***

red   blue   black   yellow   green   orange

K **Listen and repeat. Practice.**

A: What color is your shirt?

B: It's blue.

L **Practice. Say the color. Get into groups.**

My shirt is blue.

M **Write *red, blue,* and *black.***

red

blue

black

N **Spell.**

A: Spell *too.*   **A:** Spell *red.*   **A:** Spell *blue.*   **A:** Spell *black.*

B: t...o...o   **B:** r...e...d   **B:** b...l...u...e   **B:** b...l...a...c...k

O **Listen. Track the words.**

Yasmine lives in Arizona. She wears yellow and black a lot. Yellow is her favorite color.

P **Underline *Y*, *y*, and *bl*.**
Circle color words.

Q **Listen and circle.**

1. What is Yasmine's favorite color?

   a. yellow   b. black

2. Where does Yasmine live?

   a. Arizona   b. black

R **Listen and repeat. Write.**

I am wearing a yellow shirt.
Yellow is my favorite color.
I like blue too.

S **Write.**

I am wearing a _____ shirt.

_____ is my favorite color.

I like _____ too.

To the Store t

$$t = t$$

A Listen and repeat.

t   t   t   t

B Listen and repeat.

hat

coat

pants

belt

shirts

T-shirts

C Listen and repeat. Circle words with *t*.

1.

(2.)

3.

4.

5.

6.

7.

8.

9.

D Circle *T* and *t*.

t	f	T	(t)	f	t	⊥	f	t
t	t	f	T	t	⊥	t	T	f
t	f	t	f	T	t	f	t	⊥

E Write *t*.

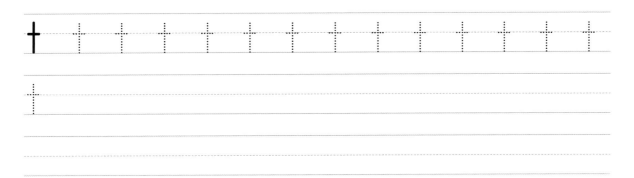

F Listen and repeat. Write *t*.

1. __t__ea
2. ____runk
3. blanke____

4. bel____
5. ____ie
6. ha____

G Write *T*.

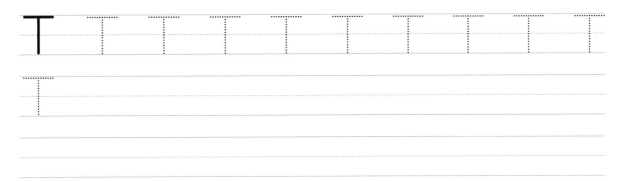

H Listen and repeat. Write *T*.

1. **T**-shirts are $12 each.

   ____-shirts are $12 each.

2. **T**om buys two shirts.

   ____om buys two shirts.

I Listen and repeat.

A: How many pairs of shoes are on the shelf?

B: 15.

how   many

J Practice with *shirts* and *pairs of pants*.

K Listen and repeat.

A: How many shoes are in your closet?

B: 3 pairs.

10 (ten)	16 (sixteen)
11 (eleven)	17 (seventeen)
12 (twelve)	18 (eighteen)
13 (thirteen)	19 (nineteen)
14 (fourteen)	20 (twenty)
15 (fifteen)	

L Write *how* and *many*.

how

many

M Spell.

A: Spell *how*.

B: *h…o…w*

A: Spell *many*.

B: *m…a…n…y*

A: Spell *too*.

B: *t…o…o*

A: Spell *red*.

B: *r…e…d*

A: Spell *blue*.

B: *b…l…u…e*

A: Spell *black*.

B: *b…l…a…c…k*

N Play. Who can spell more words?

O Listen. Track the words.

Tilly's
02/02/2024

LIST OF PURCHASES

Description	Price
2 T-shirts	$15
1 Tennis shoes	$35
1 Coat	$50
************************	
Tax	$10
Total	$110

P Underline *T* and *t*.

Q Listen and circle.

1. How many T-shirts does he buy?

   a. 2   b. $15

2. What is the tax?

   a. total   b. $10

R Write how many.

In My Closet

_____ T-shirts   _____ pairs of pants

_____ shirts   _____ pairs of shorts

_____ pairs of shoes

_____ pairs of socks

4 How Do I Look? e

A **Listen and repeat.**

e   e   e   e

B **Listen and repeat.**

Eliza

jacket

necklace

belt

dress

handbag

C **Listen and repeat. Circle words with *e*.**

1. XL

2.

3.

4.

5.

6.

7.

8.

9.

D **Circle *E* and *e*.**

e	e	E	6	e	Ǝ	ə	E	e
e	6	ə	(e)	E	ə	e	ə	Ǝ

E Write *e.*

e e e e e e e e e e e

e

F Listen and repeat. Write *e.*

1. r_e_d   2. b___d   3. t___n

4. dr___ss   5. b___lt   6. jack___t

G Write *E.*

E E E E E E E E E E

E

H Listen and repeat. Write *E* and *e.*

1. **Ed** likes **r**ed shirts.

___d likes r___d shirts.

2. **E**xtra-large shirts are over there.

___xtra-large shirts are over th___re.

I Listen and repeat.

A: What size shirt do you need?

B: Extra-large.

small
large

J Practice with *dress* and *jacket*.

K Listen and repeat.

A: What size jacket do you need?

B: Small.

Size Chart			
small	medium	large	extra-large
S	M	L	XL

L Practice with *medium, large,* and *extra-large*.

M Write *small* and *large*.

small

large

N Spell.

A: Spell *small*

B: s...m...a...l...l

A: Spell *blue*.

B: b...l...u...e

A: Spell *large*.

B: l...a...r...g...e

A: Spell *black*.

B: b...l...a...c...k

A: Spell *too*.

B: t...o...o

A: Spell *how*.

B: h...o...w

A: Spell *red*.

B: r...e...d

A: Spell *many*.

B: m...a...n...y

O **Listen. Track the words.**

Edwin wants an extra-large jacket. Jackets are expensive. He needs ten more dollars.

P **Underline _E_ and _e_.**

> $ = cheap
>
> $$$$ = expensive

Q **Listen and circle.**

1. What does Edwin want?

   a. jackets   b. a jacket

2. What does Edwin need?

   a. a jacket   b. ten dollars

R **Listen and repeat. Write.**

I want shoes, socks, and a jacket.
I need more money.
I need $10.

S **Write.**

I want _____, _____,

and a _____.

I need more money.

I need $_____.

Save Five Dollars! v

A Listen and repeat.

v   v   v   v

B Listen and repeat.

Vitality Clothing			
Pants	**Dresses**	**Vests**	**Visors**
$45 save $5	$65 save $7	$30 save $8	$12 save $8

C Listen and repeat. Circle words with *v*.

1.

2.

3.

4.

5.

6.

7.

8.

9.

D Circle *v*.

v	w	(v)	u	y	^	v	w	y
v	u	^	w	v	y	^	v	u
v	v	y	v	^	v	y	^	v

E Write *v*.

V   V   V   V   V   V   V   V   V   V   V   V   V

V

F Listen and repeat. Write *v*.

1. __v__ase   2. ___isor   3. lo___e

4. ___an   5. se___en   6. tele___ision

G Write *V*.

V   V   V   V   V   V   V   V   V   V   V   V

V

H Listen and repeat. Write *V*.

1. **V**egetables are delicious.

___egetables are delicious.

2. Her best friend is **V**ictoria.

Her best friend is ___ictoria.

I Listen and repeat.

How much are the vests?

Twenty-five dollars.

how	much

J Practice with *pants, dresses,* and *visors.*

K Listen and repeat.

A: How much are the pants?

B: Twenty-five dollars.
Save five dollars!

21 (twenty-one)	26 (twenty-six)
22 (twenty-two)	27 (twenty-seven)
23 (twenty-three)	28 (twenty-eight)
24 (twenty-four)	29 (twenty-nine)
25 (twenty-five)	30 (thirty)

L Practice with *vests, dresses,* and *visors.*

M Write *how* and *much.*

how

much

N Spell.

A: Spell *much.*   **A:** Spell *small.*   **A:** Spell *large.*   **A:** Spell *how.*

B: m…u…c…h   **B:** s…m…a…l…l   **B:** l…a…r…g…e   **B:** h…o…w

O Practice.

P Listen. Track the words.

Vitality Clothing			
Pants	**Dresses**	**Vests**	**Visors**
$45	$65	$30	$12
save $5	save $7	save $8	save $8

Q Underline *V* and *v*. Circle *save*.

R Listen and circle.

1. How much do you save on dresses?　　a. $65　　b. $7

2. How much are the visors?　　a. $12　　b. $8

S Listen.

Turvel Clothing		
Pants	Dresses	Vests
Regular: $22	Regular: $55	Regular: $22
Sale: $20	Sale: $45	Sale: $17

T Write.

Turvel Clothing		
Pants	Dresses	Vests
Regular: $22	Regular: $55	Regular: $22
Sale: $20	Sale: $45	Sale: $17
Save: $_____	_____: $_____	_____: $_____

A Circle.

~~too~~
red
blue
black
how
much
many
small
large

a	e	b	s	o	m	e	u	i	k
m	u	l	n	b	t	m	u	c	h
a	y	u	i	m	o	a	e	t	i
y	r	e	d	y	o	n	x	h	l
b	e	q	t	u	e	y	v	o	i
e	q	z	d	r	s	u	o	w	o
p	t	c	d	f	m	e	l	u	f
c	f	r	w	l	a	r	g	e	g
o	i	y	t	b	l	a	c	k	k
b	n	e	x	t	l	e	h	k	p
x	d	e	w	q	a	x	h	y	r
z	v	g	r	e	x	n	k	l	o

B Write letters. Make words.

too
red
blue
black
how
much
many
small
large

C Write *a* and *the*.

a a a a a a a a a a a

a

the the the the the the the

the

D Listen and repeat.

1. ____ shirt

2. ____ hat

3. ____ dress

4. ____ pair of shoes

5. ____ pair of pants

6. ____ pair of shorts

E Listen and repeat.

1. _____ visor

2. _____ jacket

3. _____ tie

4. _____ shoes

5. _____ pants

6. _____ shorts

I need **a** shirt. I want **the** red shirt!

F Practice.

Name	What are you wearing?
Federico	*a red shirt, black pants, black shoes*

G Write *the* and *wearing*.

the	**wearing**

the

wearing

H Spell.

A: Spell *much*.   **A:** Spell *size*.   **A:** Spell *how*.   **A:** Spell *many*.

B: m…u…c…h   **B:** s…i…z…e   **B:** h…o….w   **B:** m…a…n…y

A: Spell *too*.   **A:** Spell *yellow*.   **A:** Spell *blue*.   **A:** Spell *black*.

B: t…o…o   **B:** y…e…l…l…o…w   **B:** b…l…u…e   **B:** b…l…a…c…k

A: Spell *the*.   **A:** Spell *wearing*.

B: t…h…e   **B:** w…e…a…r…i…n…g

I Listen. Track the words.

Victor is wearing black pants and a blue shirt.
The black pants are extra-large, and the shirt is too.
He needs shoes.

J Circle *the*, *black*, *blue*, and *too*.

K Listen. Circle.

1. What color are his pants?
   a. blue   b. black

2. What does he need?
   a. shoes   b. a blue shirt

L Write.

I am wearing black pants and a red shirt.
The black pants are medium, and the shirt is
too. I need a hat.

M Write.

I am wearing _____ pants

and a _____ shirt.

The _____ pants are medium,

and the shirt is _____. I need

a _____.

Quiz

A Listen and circle.

sh 1. a.    b.    c.

y 2. a.   b.   c.

bl 3. a.   b.   c.

t 4. a.   b.   c.

e 5. a.   b.   c.

v 6. a.   b.   c.

B Listen. Write.

1. ___orts
2. ___arn
3. ___ ___ue
4. ___-shirt
5. dr___ss
6. sa___e

C Listen. Write.

1. He is wearing ___ ___ack ___ ___oes.

2. The jack___t is ___xtra-large.

3. ___ellow is my favorite color.

5 Community

Look at the signs. What do they mean?

Point to the Stop sign.   Point to the No Parking sign.

Point to the bus sign.

1 The City c

A **Listen and repeat.** c   c   c   c / c   c   c   c

B **Listen and repeat.**

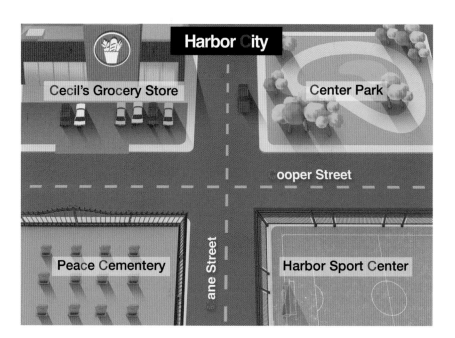

C **Listen and check the sound you hear.**

		k sound	s sound
1. bicycle			✓
3. carrot			
5. pencil			

		k sound	s sound
2. car			
4. face			
6. juice			

D **Circle c.**

c	(c)	o	u	c	o	c	o	u
c	o	u	c	o	c	u	c	o

E Write *c*.

C c c c c c c c c c c c c c

c

F Listen and repeat. Write *c*.

1. _c_ir__le

2. ____an

3. ____oat

4. ____ity

5. ____ell phone

6. ____ereal

G Write *C*.

C C C C C C C C C C

C

H Listen and repeat. Write *C*.

1. Cecilia lives in New York City.

____ecilia lives in New York

____ity.

2. Carrots are $3 at Cooper's Market.

____arrots are $3

at ____ooper's Market.

I Listen and repeat.

A: Where's Harbor Sport Center?

B: It's in Harbor City.

J Practice with a partner.

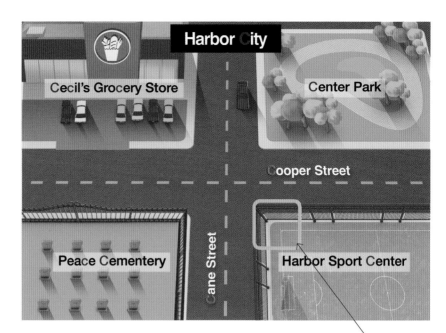

K Listen and repeat.

A: Where's <u>Harbor Sport Center</u>?

B: It's on the corner of Cooper and Cane Street.

L Practice with other places.

M Write *corner* and *of*.

corner corner

of of

N Spell.

corner	of	circle	where
live	in	on	the

O Ask about places where you live.

P **Listen. Track the words.**

I live in Palm City on Main Street. Celia lives in Palm City on First Street.

Ahmed lives in Palm City on Center Street. Lucy lives in Palm City on Center Street too.

Q **Underline** C. **Circle** *in*, *on*, *live*, **and** *lives*.

R **Listen and circle.**

1. What city do they all live in?
a. Palm City   b. Ahmed and Lucy

2. Who lives on Center Street?
a. Palm City   b. Ahmed and Lucy

S **Write.**

I live in Palm City on Main Street. Celia lives in Palm City on First Street. Ahmed lives in Palm City on Center Street. Lucy lives in Palm City on Center Street too.

T **Write about you and a partner.**

I live in _____

on _____.

_____ lives in

_____ on

_____.

2 Please Give Me Directions   r

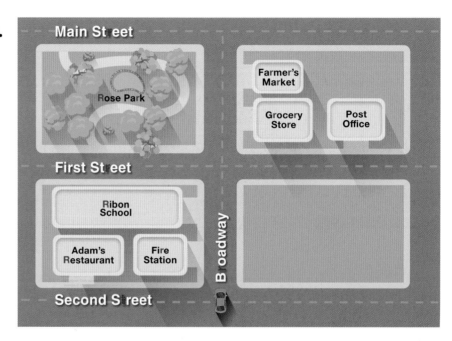

A **Listen and repeat.**   *r*   *r*   *r*   *r*

B **Listen and repeat.**

Main Street

Rose Park

Farmer's Market

Grocery Store

Post Office

First Street

Ribon School

Adam's Restaurant

Fire Station

Broadway

Second Street

C **Listen. Check *r* or *w*.**

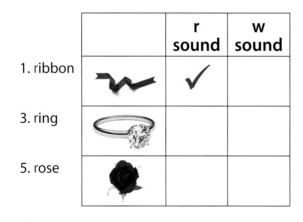

		r sound	w sound
1. ribbon		✓	
3. ring			
5. rose			

		r sound	w sound
2. watch			
4. wall			
6. radio			

D **Circle *r*.**

r	ⓡ	r	ſ	r	ɬ	l	r	ɬ
r	ɿ	ɬ	r	ſ	r	r	ſ	r

E Write *r*.

r r r r r r r r r r r r r

r

F Listen and repeat. Write *r*.

1. fi__r__e

2. ma____ket

3. bu____ge____

4. pa____k

5. sto____e

6. mothe____

G Write *R*.

R R R R R R R R R R R

R

H Listen and repeat. Write *R* and *r*.

1. Rosa works at a store.

____osa wo____ks at a sto____e.

2. Restaurants are expensive here.

____estau____ants a____e
expensive he____e.

I Listen and repeat.

A: Where's the Fire Station?

B: It's on Broadway.

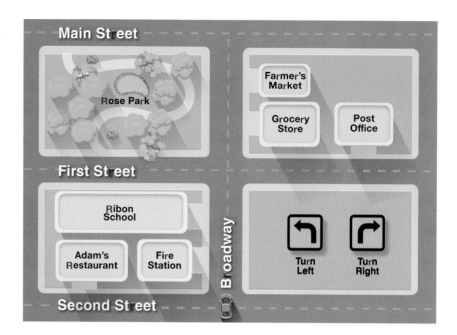

J Practice with other students.

turn   left   right

K Listen and repeat.

A: Please give me directions to the <u>post office</u>.

B: OK, turn right on First Street.

L Practice with *Ribbon School*, *Farmer's Market*, *Grocery Store*, and *Fire Station*.

M Write *turn*, *left*, and *right*.

N Spell *corner, of, turn, left, right, where, please, on,* and *the*.

O **Listen. Track the words.**

Ruben lives in Rolling Hills, California. From the school, go west on Crest Road and turn right on Buggy Whip Drive.

P **Underline *R* and *r*. Circle *turn*, *right*, and *lives*.**

Q **Listen and circle.**

1. What city does Ruben live in?
   a. Rolling Hills
   b. Buggy Whip Drive

2. What way do you turn?
   a. right
   b. left

R **Listen. Write.**

I go to Lee County Adult School.

The school is on Broadway.

S **Write.**

I _____ _____ Lee County Adult School.

The school is _____ Broadway

T **Write about you.**

I go to _____.

The school is on _____.

3 Transportation *tr*

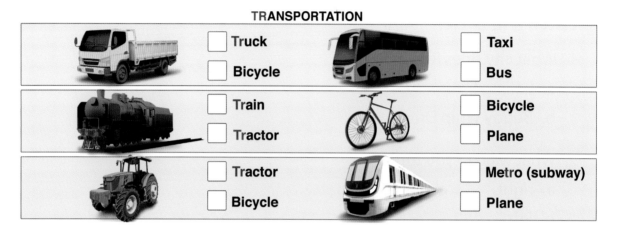

A **Listen and repeat.** *tr*   *tr*   *tr*   *tr*

B **Listen and repeat. Check.**

TRANSPORTATION

☐ Truck	☐ Taxi	
☐ Bicycle	☐ Bus	
☐ Train	☐ Bicycle	
☐ Tractor	☐ Plane	
☐ Tractor	☐ Metro (subway)	
☐ Bicycle	☐ Plane	

C **Listen and check *t* or *tr*.**

		t sound	tr sound
1. train			✓
3. T-shirt			
5. two			
7. triangle			

		t sound	tr sound
2. tie			
4. tree			
6. trash can			
8. tractor			

D **Circle *t* and *r*.**

t	ⓣ	ⓡ	ɿ	t	ƚ	r	t	ɿ
r	r	t	ɿ	ƚ	r	ƚ	ɿ	t

E Write *tr*.

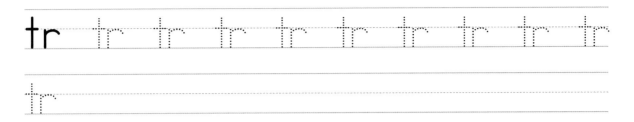

F Listen and repeat. Write *tr*.

 1. __tr__ain

 2. _____am car

 3. _____actor

 4. _____ack

 5. _____uck

 6. me_____o

G Write *Tr*.

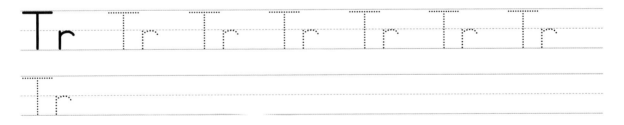

H Listen and repeat. Write *Tr*.

1. Trains run all day.

_____ains run all day.

2. Tran takes the bus.

_____an takes the bus.

I **Listen and repeat.**

A: How do you go to work?

B: I go by train.

J **Practice with other students.**

K **Listen and repeat.**

A: How do you go to school?

B: I go <u>by train</u>.

I go by train.
I go by car.
I go by bus.
I go by bicycle.
I walk.

by   work

L **Practice with other students.**

M **Write** *by* **and** *work*.

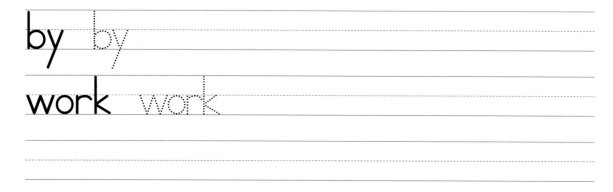

N **Say the word. Spell it.**

corner	of	turn	left	right
by	work	circle	where	go

O Listen. Track the words.

TRANSPORTATION TO WORK: IN HARBOR CITY

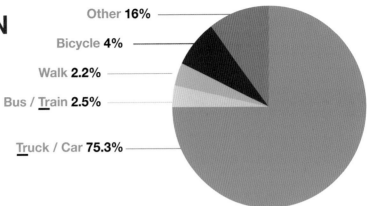

Other **16%**

Bicycle **4%**

Walk **2.2%**

Bus / Train **2.5%**

Truck / Car **75.3%**

P Underline *Tr*.

Q Listen and circle.

1. What percent (%) of people go to work by bicycle? a. 40% b. 4%

2. What percent (%) of people walk to work? a. 2.2% b. 22%

R Listen. Write.

I walk to school. Armando goes to school by car.

S Write.

I _____ to _____.

Armando _____ to _____

_____ _____.

A Listen and repeat.   *y*   *y*   *y*   *y*

B Listen and repeat.

C Listen and check.

		y in family	y in yellow
1. balcony		✓	
3. key			
5. penny			
7. yogurt			

		y in family	y in yellow
2. yarn			
4. yoga			
6. baby			
8. yoyo			

D Circle *y*.

y	(y)	v	g	v	y	v	g	y
y	g	y	v	y	v	y	v	g

E Write *y*.

y y y y y y y y y y y y

y

F Listen and repeat. Write *y*.

 1. bab__y__

 2. famil_____

 3. ke_____

 4. dais_____

 5. happ_____

 6. grann_____

G Listen. Write *y*.

Amy has a happ _____ famil _____. She lives in
New York Cit _____ in an apartment. She is married.
They have a son and a bab _____.

H Listen and repeat.

Country   City   Suburbs

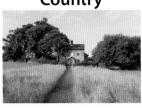 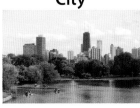 

A: Do you live in the city?

B: No, I live in the country.

yes   no

I Practice with *country* and *suburbs*.

J Listen and repeat. Then practice with your information.

A: Do you live in the suburbs?

B: Yes, I do.

K Write *yes* and *no*.

yes   yes

no   no

L Spell a word. Your partner says the word.

corner	happy	left	like	no	right
small	turn	work	yes	your	

M Practice.

N **Listen. Track the words.**

Mary's house has two bedrooms and two bathrooms. It is in the suburbs. She has a small family.

O **Underline** *y*. **Circle** *small* **and** *family*.

P **Listen and circle.**

1. Mary lives in the city.   a. True   b. False

2. Mary has a large family.   a. True   b. False

Q **Listen. Write.**

I live in a house. It has three bedrooms and two bathrooms. It is in the suburbs. I have a small family.

R **Circle.**

I live / lives in a house.

It has three / tree bedrooms and two bathrooms.

It is on / in the suburbs.

I have an / a small family.

Housing Ads   th

A **Listen and repeat.** *th*   *th*   *th*   *th*

B **Listen and repeat.**

> For Rent
>
> Three-bedroom, two-bathroom house.
> 234 Third Lane, North Chicago. Call Theo, 312 232 3334.

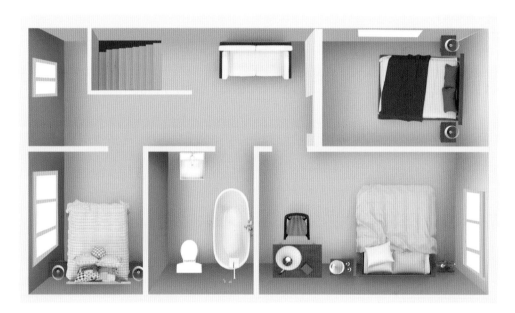

C **Listen and check *th* or *t*.**

		th	t
1. tree			✓
3. tie			
5. thirteen	**13**		
7. south			

		th	t
2. three	**3**		
4. table			
6. bathroom			
8. ten	**10**		

D Write *th*.

E Listen and repeat. Write *th*.

1. __th__ree

2. tee_____

3. clo_____

4. ba_____room

5. _____umb

6. _____igh

F Mime a word. Guess the word.

G Write *Th*.

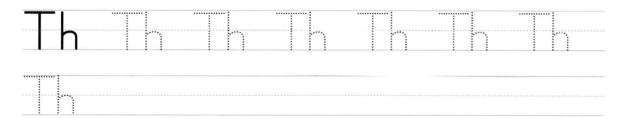

H Listen and repeat. Write *Th*.

1. Thank you for your help!

_____ank you for your help!

2. The class is on Thursday.

The class is on _____ursday.

I **Listen and repeat.**

A: We need a three-bedroom house with two bathrooms.

B: Maybe three bathrooms!

(with)

J **Practice with a partner.**

K **Listen and repeat.**

A: How many bedrooms and bathrooms do you have?

B: We have two bedrooms and one bathroom.

L **Practice with your own information.**

M **Write** *with*.

N **Spell the words with a partner. Take turns.**

corner	of	turn	left	right	by
work	yes	no	with	spell	happy
you	and	how	many		

O Listen. Track the words.

House 1	Apartment 2	House 3
For Rent **Bedrooms:** 2 **Bathrooms:** 2 **City:** North Chicago **Call:** 312 555 1345	**For Rent** **Bedrooms:** 1 **Bathrooms:** 1 **City:** North Chicago **Call:** 312 555 4455	**For Rent** **Bedrooms:** 4 **Bathrooms:** 2 **City:** North Chicago **Call:** 312 555 2314

P Underline *th*. Circle the number with the *th* sound.

Q Listen and circle.

1. How many bedrooms does #1 have?

a. 1

b. 2

c. 3

2. How many bathrooms does #3 have?

a. 1

b. 2

c. 3

R Write.

Housing	Bathrooms	Bedrooms
House 1	2 bathrooms	2 bedrooms
Apartment 2		
House 3		

A Circle.

~~corner~~	r	e	h	r	x	w	o	r	k	l	s	h	o	c	u	e
of	r	e	t	t	u	r	n	u	f	y	m	p	f	g	a	k
turn	q	l	k	h	n	i	q	g	u	i	b	y	o	t	u	w
	f	e	e	t	o	g	e	c	f	s	x	e	r	l	e	j
left	q	v	t	s	m	h	c	d	i	i	t	s	g	o	t	r
right	f	i	b	b	w	t	q	w	p	s	s	j	g	x	s	r
by	d	a	b	m	l	n	u	n	q	e	r	b	s	p	h	a
work	t	m	n	b	i	o	y	p	g	q	y	r	a	d	d	u
	w	r	x	q	g	t	j	g	t	i	u	t	t	m	n	p
yes	z	i	o	o	y	a	x	s	l	y	u	m	y	b	v	k
no	q	p	f	k	i	g	p	n	d	a	w	i	t	h	l	e
with	c	o	r	n	e	r	l	e	f	t	q	f	v	w	h	x

B Write the words.

corner
of
turn
left
right
by
work
yes
no
with

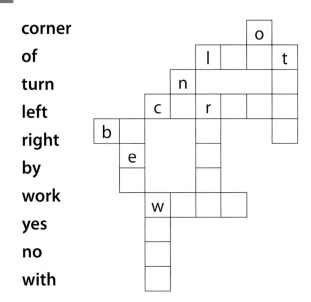

C Write *ou*.

ou ou ou ou ou ou ou ou ou

ou

D Listen and repeat. Write *ou*.

1. cl_____d

2. h_____r

3. h_____se

4. m_____se

5. m_____th

6. s_____th

E **Listen and repeat.**

I	**have**	a house.	I have a house.
It	**has**	three bedrooms.	It has three bedrooms.

F **Write** *have* **and** *has*.

have have

has has

G **Write** *have* **or** *has*.

1. I _____ an apartment.

2. My apartment _____ three bedrooms and one bathroom.

3. I _____ a house.

4. My house _____ two bedrooms.

H **Spell.**

by	corner	has	have	left	no
of	right	turn	with	work	yes

I Ask a partner. Write.

What city do you live in?

Please spell it. _____

J Ask a partner. Write.

What street do you live on?

Please spell it. _____

K Give directions. Say *turn right* or *turn left*.

End here

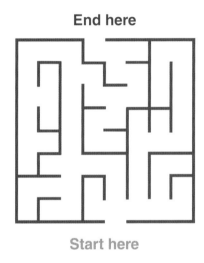

Start here

L Ask a partner. Write.

How do you go to school?   By _____

M Ask a partner. Write.

How many bedrooms do you have?

I have _____ bedroom(s).

How many bathrooms do you have?

I have _____ bathroom(s).

Quiz

A **Listen and circle.**

c 1. a.    b.    c.

r 2. a.    b.   c.

tr 3. a.   b.   c.

y 4. a.   b.   c.

th 5. a.   b.   c.

B **Write.**

1. turn _____ight   2. cit_____   3. bi_____ycle   4. _____ain   5. wi_____

C **Write.**

by	corner	left	of	with

1. I go to work _____ car.

2. It's on the _____ _____ First and Broadway.

3. I want a house _____ three bedrooms.

4. Turn _____ on Main Street.

D Write. Give directions.

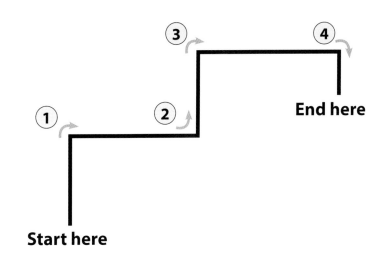

1. <u>Turn right.</u>

2. _____

3. _____

4. _____

Start here

End here

E Read.

1

House

3 bedrooms

2 bathrooms

1,500 square feet

New kitchen

Call: 714 555 3765

2

Apartment

2 bedrooms

1 bathroom

Call: 213 555 8987

3

House

1 bedroom

1 bathroom

In the country

Call: 559 555 3731

F Write.

	House or Apartment	Bedrooms	Bathrooms	Phone Number
1.	*house*	*3*	*2*	*714 555 3765*
2.				
3.				

6 Health

Look. Choose three signs. What do they mean?

1 Sleep Well!   s

A **Listen and repeat.**   s   s   s   s / s   s   s   s

B **Listen and repeat.**

─────────────── **Healthy Living** ───────────────

Sleep 7-8 hours

Exercise 30 minutes

Eat three meals

C **Listen and repeat. Check words with the s and z sounds.**

	s sound	z sound
1. exercise	☐	✓
3. sun	☐	☐
5. shoes	☐	☐
7. trees	☐	☐

	s sound	z sound
2. sandwich	☐	☐
4. hours	☐	☐
6. meals	☐	☐
8. seven	☐	☐

D Write *s*.

S s s s s s s s s s s s

s

E Listen and repeat. Write *s*.

1. _s_ock _s_

2. ___oap

3. ___tar

4. shoe___

5. exerci___e

6. orange___

F Write *S*.

S S S S S S S S S S S

S

G Listen and repeat. Write *S* and *s*.

1. **S**am like**s** apple**s**.

___am like___ apple___.

2. **S**leep **s**even to eight hour**s** a day.

___leep ___even to eight hour___ a day.

H Listen and repeat.

A: How many hours do you <u>work</u> a day?

B: I <u>work</u> four hours a day. I work twenty hours a week.

I Practice with *exercise* and *sleep*.

day   week

J Write about three students.

Name	How many hours do you sleep a day?	How many hours do you exercise a week?
Sam	8 hours	3 hours

K Write *day* and *week*.

day

week

L Spell a word. Your partner says the word.

day   week   close   sorry   please   for   too   have

M **Listen. Track the words.**

Isaac's Schedule

Tuesday	
7 AM	Exercise
8 AM	Breakfast
10 AM	School
12 PM	Lunch
1 PM	Work
6 PM	Dinner
10 PM	Sleep

1 day	1 week
2 days	3 weeks

N **Listen. Track the words.**

Sally exercises four hours a week.
She sleeps eight hours a day.
Ned exercises two hours a week.
He sleeps six hours a day.

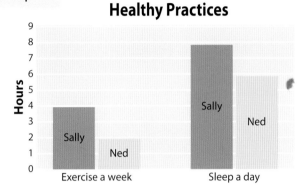

Healthy Practices

O **Underline** *S* **and** *s*. **Circle** *day* **and** *week*.

P **Listen and circle.**

1. Who sleeps more, Sally or Ned? a. Sally b. Ned

2. Who exercises more, Sally or Ned? a. Sally b. Ned

Q **Listen.**

I sleep eight hours a day. I exercise four hours a week. I eat three meals a day.

R **Circle the correct answer.**

1. i / I sleep eight hours a day.

2. I exercise four hour / hours a week.

3. I eat three meals / meal a day.

S **Write about you.**

I sleep _____ hours a day.

I exercise _____ hours a week.

I _____.

2 A Cold

A Listen and repeat.

o   o   o   o

B Listen and repeat.

Cold

sore throat

runny nose

headache

C Listen and check.

	o sound	a sound
1.	✓	

2. o sound ☐ a sound ☐

3. o sound ☐ a sound ☐

4. o sound ☐ a sound ☐

5. o sound ☐ a sound ☐

6.  o sound ☐ a sound ☐

7. o sound ☐ a sound ☐

8. o sound ☐ a sound ☐

D Write o.

O ⚬ ⚬ ⚬ ⚬ ⚬ ⚬ ⚬ ⚬ ⚬ ⚬ ⚬

○

E Listen and repeat. Write o.

1.  n_o_se

2. c___at

3.  b___w

4.  r___se

5.  b___at

6. wind___w

F Write O.

○ ○ ○ ○ ○ ○ ○ ○ ○

○

G Listen and repeat. Write O and o.

1. **O**livia has a c**o**ld.

____livia has a c____ld.

2. **O**mar is very sick.

____mar is very sick.

H Listen and repeat.

A: I have a <u>runny nose</u>.

B: Maybe you have a cold.

I Practice with *sore throat* and *headache*.

feel	maybe

J Listen and repeat.

A: I feel sick.

B: Oh, I'm sorry.

A: I have a runny nose and a sore throat too.

B: Maybe you need to stay home today.

K Practice with other students.

L Write *maybe* and *feel*.

maybe

feel

M Spell.

maybe feel open sorry please for too have day week

N Listen. Track the words.

Rosa

She has a sore throat.

Omar

He has a runny nose.

Me

I have a headache.

O Underline *O* and *o*. Circle *have* and *has*.

P Listen and circle.

1. What's the matter with Omar?

   a. He has a headache.   b. He has a runny nose.

2. What's the matter with Rosa?

   a. He has a sore throat.   b. She has a sore throat.

Q Listen and repeat.

I	**have**	a headache	I have a headache.
He She	**has**	a runny nose a sore throat	He has a runny nose. She has a sore throat.

R Write *have* or *has*.

1. I _____ a sore throat.

2. She _____ a runny nose.

3. He _____ a headache.

S Guess the symptom.

3 I'm Sick! *ch*

A **Listen and repeat.**   *ch*   *ch*   *ch*   *ch / ch*   *ch*   *ch*   *ch*

B **Listen and repeat.**

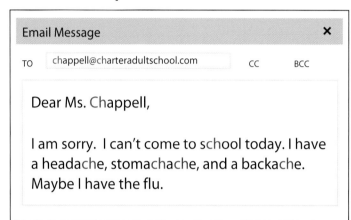

Email Message   ✕

TO   chappell@charteradultschool.com   CC   BCC

Dear Ms. Chappell,

I am sorry. I can't come to school today. I have
a headache, stomachache, and a backache.
Maybe I have the flu.

stomachache

backache

C **Listen and repeat. Check words with the *ch* and *k* sounds.**

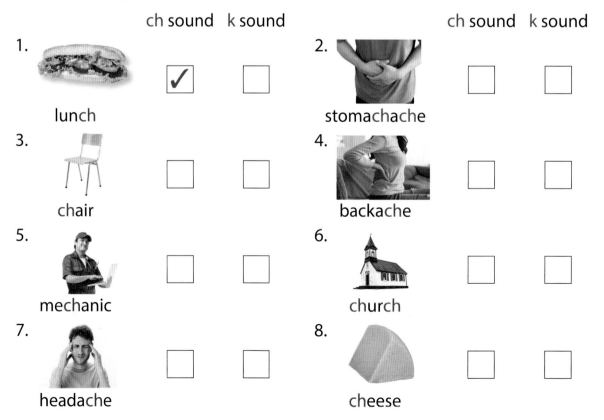

	ch sound	k sound		ch sound	k sound
1. lunch	✓	☐	2. stomachache	☐	☐
3. chair	☐	☐	4. backache	☐	☐
5. mechanic	☐	☐	6. church	☐	☐
7. headache	☐	☐	8. cheese	☐	☐

D Write *ch*.

ch ch ch ch ch ch ch ch

ch

E Listen and repeat. Write *ch*.

1.

____ch____ocolate

2.

_____ips

3.

_____ick

4.

stoma_____ache

5.

me_____anic

6.

s_____ool

F Write *Ch*.

Ch Ch Ch Ch Ch Ch Ch Ch

Ch

G Listen and repeat. Write *Ch* and *ch*.

1. **Ch**iropractors help backa**ch**es.

_____iropractors help backa_____es.

2. **Ch**arlie is a doctor.

_____arlie is a doctor.

H Listen and repeat.

Name	Problem	Date	Time
Chloe Simms	flu symptoms	3-25	2:30
			3:00
Samuel Autor	a backache		3:30
Charlie Johnson	a stomachache		4:00

A: Hello, I need an appointment to see the doctor.

B: What's the problem?

A: I have a bad stomachache.

I Practice with *backache* and *sore throat*.

can't	later	problem

J Listen and repeat.

B: Can you come in at 3:00 PM?

A: No, I can't. How about 4:00 PM?

B: Okay, see you later!

3:00	three o'clock
3:30	three thirty
4:00	four o'clock
4:30	four thirty

K Practice with other times.

L Write *can't*, *later*, and *problem*.

M Spell.

can't	later	problem	maybe	feel	spell	name	your

need   much   have   day   week

N **Listen. Track the words.**

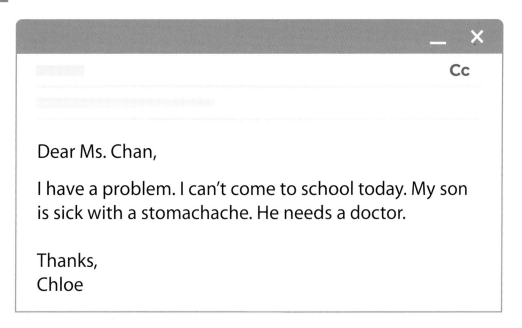

Cc

Dear Ms. Chan,

I have a problem. I can't come to school today. My son is sick with a stomachache. He needs a doctor.

Thanks,
Chloe

O **Underline** *Ch* **and** *ch*. **Circle** *can't*, *with*, **and** *problem*.

P **Listen and circle.**

1. Who is sick?

   a. Chloe   b. Chloe's son

2. Who is the student?

   a. Chloe   b. Chloe's teacher

Q **Listen. Write.**

Dear Ms. Chan, I have a problem. I can't come to school today. I am sick. See you later.

R **Write.**

Dear Ms. Chan, I have a _____.

I _____ come to school today. I am sick.

See you _____.

4 At the Doctor's Office -ing

A Listen and repeat.   *ing   ing   ing   ing*

B Listen and repeat.

talking   sitting   **Waiting Room**   listening   writing   reading

C Listen and check.

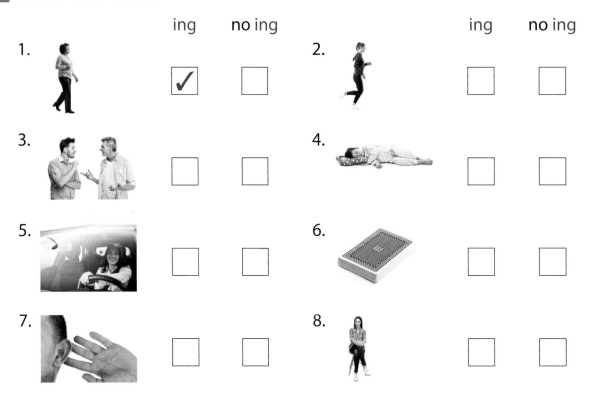

	ing	no ing			ing	no ing
1.	✓		2.			
3.			4.			
5.			6.			
7.			8.			

D Write *ing*.

ing ing ing ing ing ing ing

ing

E Listen and repeat. Write *ing*.

1.  walk__ing__

2. driv_____

3. listen_____

4. runn_____

5. kick_____

6. talk_____

F Listen. Track the words.

I	am	talking	I am talking.
He She	is	talking	He is talking. She is talking.
They	are	talking	They are talking.

G Listen. Write *ing*.

1. He is talk _____ on the phone.

2. The receptionist is writ _____.

3. They are sitt _____ in the waiting room.

4. Two women are read _____.

H Listen and repeat.

Doctor: Who is next?

Receptionist: Mr. Mora. He is waiting in the exam room.

I Listen and repeat.

Doctor: How are you, Mr. Mora?

Mr. Mora: I have a headache.

Doctor: Oh, I'm sorry. You have a fever, also.

Mr. Mora: Can you help me?

Doctor: Yes, of course.

who	next

J Practice with *stomachache*, *backache*, **and** *sore throat*.

K Write *who* and *next*.

who

next

L Spell.

who	next	can't	later	problem	maybe	feel	open
where	please	need	many	have	day	week	

M **Listen. Track the words.**

Six patients are in the waiting room. Five are sitting down. A man is talking on the phone. Two women are reading. Two men are talking to Mr. Mora.

N **Underline** *ing*.

O **Listen and circle.**

1. How many patients are in the waiting room?

   a. 3   b. 6   c. 8

2. How many people are sitting?

   a. 2   b. 3   c. 5

P **Listen and write.**

I am sitting in the waiting room. I am reading. My husband is here too. He is talking to Mr. Mora. I am waiting for my appointment with the doctor.

Q **Write the missing words.**

I _____ sitting in the waiting room. I am _____. My husband is here _____. He _____ talking to Mr. Mora. I _____ _____ for my appointment with the doctor.

Medicine i

A Listen and repeat. *i* *i* *i* *i*

B Listen and repeat. Match.

_____ 1. Antacid tablets are big pills. They are for stomach problems.

a.

_____ 2. Cough syrup is a liquid. It is for a sore throat or a cough.

b.

_____ 3. Aspirin is a small tablet. It is for headaches.

c.

C Listen and repeat. Check words with the *i* and *a* sound.

		i in *six*	a in *hat*			i in *six*	a in *hat*
1.		✓	☐	2.		☐	☐
3.		☐	☐	4.		☐	☐
5.		☐	☐	6.		☐	☐
7.		☐	☐	8.		☐	☐

D Write *i*.

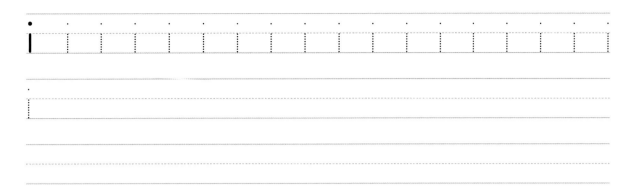

E Listen and repeat. Write *i*.

1.   p_i_g

2.   p____ll

3.   l____p

4.   st____ck

5. **6** s____x

6.   ch____ps

F Practice. Guess the word.

G Write *I*.

I = I

H Listen and repeat. Write *I* and *i*.

1. It's a good day.

    ____t's a good day.

2. Immanuel is my friend.

    ____mmanuel ____s my friend.

I Listen and repeat.

A: Take two tablets and talk to me in the morning.

B: Thank you doctor.

J Practice with a partner.

> some   take

K Listen and repeat.

A: I think I need some medicine.

B: What's the problem?

A: I have a <u>headache</u>.

B: Take some <u>aspirin</u>.

L Practice with *stomachache* and *cough*.

M Write *some* and *take*.

take

N Spell.

> some   take   who   next   can't   later   problem   maybe
> feel   listen   from   in   need   large   has

O Play. Hit the word you hear in **N**.

P Listen. Track the words.

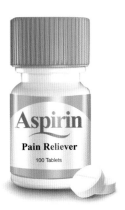

> **Instructions:** Take two pills every four hours. Do not take more than six pills in 24 hours.

Q Underline *I* and *i*. Circle *Take* and *take*.

R Listen and circle.

1. How many pills do you take every four hours? a. 24   b. 2   c. 6

2. How many pills do you take in 24 hours?   a. 24   b. 2   c. 6

S Listen.

aspirin

> **Instructions:** Take two pills every four hours. Do not take more than six pills in 24 hours.

cough syrup

> **Instructions:** Take two teaspoons every four hours.

antacid

> **Instructions:** Take two tablets every four hours. Do not take more than six tablets in 24 hours.

T Write.

Medicine	How Many ____
Aspirin	two pills
Cough Syrup	
Antacid	

U Write the names of the medications you have at home.

Put It Together   s, o, ch, ing, i

A Find and circle the words on the list.

a	e	t	s	o	m	e	u	i	k
m	u	h	n	b	t	u	h	u	r
a	y	u	i	m	a	c	e	t	i
y	r	w	q	y	k	v	x	w	l
b	e	q	t	u	e	w	v	h	i
e	q	z	d	r	f	u	o	o	o
p	t	c	d	f	e	e	l	u	f
o	i	y	t	c	s	r	u	n	k
b	n	e	x	t	d	e	h	k	p
x	d	e	w	q	a	x	h	y	r
z	v	g	r	e	x	n	k	l	o
m	l	j	u	y	t	f	c	e	b
h	a	t	r	c	a	n	'	t	l
m	t	h	b	g	t	d	x	o	e
x	e	r	e	y	i	p	k	j	m
b	r	h	y	t	e	d	x	h	k
m	i	u	l	i	s	t	e	n	y

some
take
who
next
can't
later
problem
maybe
feel
listen

B Write the words.

some
take
who
next
can't
later
problem
maybe
feel
listen

C Listen and repeat.

a   a   a   a   o   o   o   o

e   e   e   e   u   u   u   u

i   i   i   i

D Write vowels.

a   a

e   e

i   i

o   o

u   u

E Listen and repeat.

	Silent e	Two Vowels		Silent e	Two Vowels

1.
cak**e**

2.
w**a**it

3.
nos**e**

4.
c**o**at

5.
plat**e**

6.
eat

7.
driv**e**

8.
bl**u**e

9.
bik**e**

F Listen and repeat.

I	**am**		I am sick.
You	**are**		You are sick.
He She	**is**	sick.	He is sick. She is sick.
They	**are**		They are sick.

G Write *am*, *is*, and *are*.

1. I _____ sick.

2. Marie _____ sick.

3. Juan and Mario _____ sick.

4. You _____ sick.

5. Omar _____ sick.

H Write *am*, *is*, and *are*.

am

is

are

I Spell.

am   is   are   some   take   who   next   can't   later
problem   maybe   feel   listen   day   week

J Listen. Track the words.

Cold Medicine

Instructions: Take 10 ml every 6 hours. Do not take more than four doses in 24 hours.

K Listen and circle.

1. How many doses can you take in a day?

   a. 24   b. 2   c. 4

2. What is the medicine for?

   a. a cold   b. 6 hours   c. 10 ml

L Write your answers.

1. How many hours do you sleep a day?

   I sleep _____ a day.

2. How many hours do you exercise a week?

   I exercise _____ a week.

3. How many meals do you eat a day?

   I eat _____ a day.

M Ask a partner. Write.

1. How many hours do you sleep a day?

   _____ sleeps _____ a day.

2. How many hours do you exercise a week?

   _____ exercises _____ a week.

3. How many meals do you eat a day?

   _____ eats _____ a day.

Quiz

A **Listen and circle.**

s 1. a.   b.    c.

s 2. a.    b.   c.

o 3. a.   b.    c.

ch 4. a.    b.    c.

ch 5. a.   b.   c.

ing 6. a.    b.    c.

i 7. a.   b.   c.

B Listen. Write.

1. _____leep

2. exerci_____e

3. no_____e

4. _____ur_____

5. s_____ool

6. wait_____

7. s_____t

C Write.

| feels   Maybe   Take   Who |

1. _____ two tablets every four hours.

2. _____ is the next patient?

3. _____ you can take some medicine.

4. He _____ sick.

D Circle.

Name	Problem	Date	Time
Farah Ali	backache	January 14	10:30 AM
Francisco Mantilla	headache	January 14	11:00 AM
Song Hong	stomachache	January 14	11:30 AM

1. What time is Farah's appointment?

    a. 10:30 AM

    b. 11:00 AM

    c. 11:30 AM

2. Who has a headache?

    a. Farah

    b. Francisco

    c. 11:00

3. What is Song's problem?

    a. 11:30

    b. January 14

    c. stomachache

Should You Click It?

A Match.

_____ 1. wifi   a. <u>click here</u>

_____ 2. link   b. 🔒

_____ 3. secure   c. 📶

_____ 4. public   d. 🔓

B How can you be safe online? Circle.

1. Do / Don't share your password.

2. Do / Don't read emails carefully.

3. Do / Don't click on links.

4. Do / Don't use public internet.

5. Do / Don't give people personal information on the phone.

C **Watch the video. Should you click it? Circle.**

1. You get a text from your bank.   Yes   No

2. You get an email from your teacher.   Yes   No

3. You are at a café with wifi.   Yes   No

4. You get a phone call. It's the police!   Yes   No

D **Read. Is it a scam? Discuss with a partner.**

> A *scam* is when someone tells you a lie to get money or information.

1. You get a text. You won a prize!

2. You find an apartment you like online. The owner asks for money—then they will show you the apartment.

3. The government calls. They want your social security number.

4. You get an email from 0sghinskynalyy6sh@mail.com.

5. You get a text message. It's from the president!

6. You get a text message. It's from your brother, but you don't know the number. He needs money.

E **Look at the situations in D. What should you do? What should you not do?**

_____ Send money.

_____ Write back.

_____ Block the number or email.

_____ Hang up.

_____ Give them what they ask for.

_____ Get a new phone number.

Your idea: _____

7 Work

Look at the cafe. What meals can you eat here?

Is it Sunday? What are two ways to open the door?

What Do You Do? er / ar

A **Listen and repeat.**

er   er   er   er / ar   ar   ar   ar

B **Listen and repeat.**

baker

student

artist

barber

carpenter

C **Listen and check.**

	er sound	ar sound
1.	✓	
3.		
5.		
7.		

	er sound	ar sound
2.		
4.		
6.		
8.		

D **Write _er_.**

er er er er er er er er er

er

E **Listen and repeat. Write _er_.**

1. moth _er_ 2. fath____ 3. work____

4. runn____ 5. serv____ 6. toast____

F **Write _ar_.**

ar ar ar ar ar ar ar ar ar

ar

G **Listen and repeat. Write _ar_.**

1. y _ar_ n 2. st____ 3. c____

4. b____n 5. ____tist 6. p____ty

H **Listen and repeat.**

A: What do you do?

B: I'm a <u>teacher</u>.

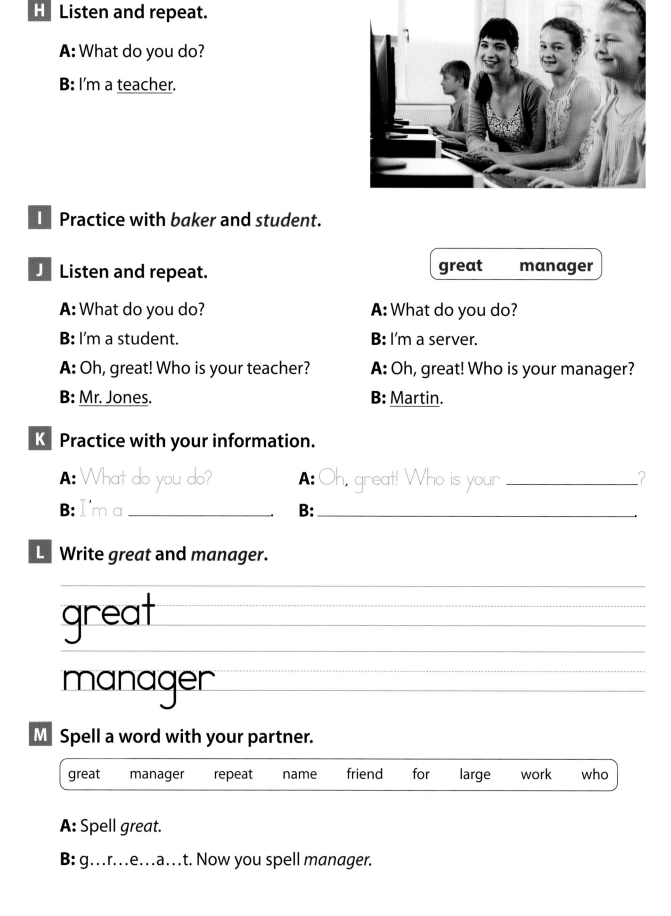

I **Practice with** *baker* **and** *student*.

J **Listen and repeat.**

great	manager

A: What do you do?

B: I'm a student.

A: Oh, great! Who is your teacher?

B: <u>Mr. Jones</u>.

A: What do you do?

B: I'm a server.

A: Oh, great! Who is your manager?

B: <u>Martin</u>.

K **Practice with your information.**

A: What do you do?

B: I'm a _____.

A: Oh, great! Who is your _____?

B: _____.

L **Write** *great* **and** *manager*.

great

manager

M **Spell a word with your partner.**

great	manager	repeat	name	friend	for	large	work	who

A: Spell *great*.

B: g…r…e…a…t. Now you spell *manager*.

N **Listen. Track the words.**

Aria is a manager at a restaurant. The restaurant is open from 11:00 AM to 10:00 PM. Aria works from 10:00 AM to 6:00 PM every day.

O **Underline** *Ar* **and** *er*. **Circle** *manager*.

P **Listen and circle.**

1. What time does Aria start work?

   a. 12 PM   b. 10 AM   c. 6 PM

2. When does the restaurant close?

   a. 12 PM   b. 10 AM   c. 10 PM

Q **Listen. Write.**

I am a student. I go to school from 3:00 PM to 5:00 PM every day. I like my class. My teacher is Mrs. Hart.

R **Circle the correct answer.**

1. I (am / is) a student.

2. I go to (skool / school) from 3:00 PM to 5:00 PM every day.

3. I (like / likes) my class.

4. My teacher (is / am) Mrs. Hart.

At Work ir / or / ur

A **Listen and repeat.**

ir   ir   ir / or   or   or / ur   ur   ur

B **Listen and repeat.**

Resume/Job History
Irma Amato Nurse Supervisor
Experience
2015 Ⓞ Assistant Nurse
2020 Ⓞ Nurse
2024 Ⓞ Nurse Supervisor

C **Listen and check.**

	ir/or/ur sound	ar sound
1.	✓	
3.		
5.		
7.		

	or/ur sound	ar sound
2.		
4.		
6.		
8.		

D Write *ur*.

ur ur ur ur ur ur ur ur ur

ur

E Listen and repeat. Write *ur*.

1. 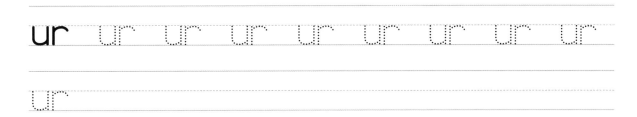 n__ur__se   2. Th____sday   3. t____n right

4. b____ger   5. Sat____day   6. p____ple

F Write *ir*.

ir ir ir ir ir ir ir ir ir ir

ir

G Listen and repeat. Write *ir*.

1. 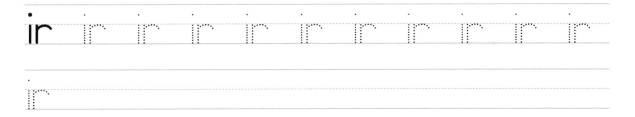 b__ir__d   2. **13** th____teen   3. sh____t

4. c____cle   5. b____thday   6. sk____t

H Listen and repeat.

A: What was your first job?

B: I was a server.

I Practice with other students.

J Listen and repeat.

A: What was your first job?

B: I was a server.

A: What do you do now?

B: I am a nurse. I work in a hospital.

was	do

K Practice with students.

L Write *was* and *do*.

was

do

M Spell.

was	do	great	manager	spell	first	go	like	too	have	am

N Practice. Act a job out. Your partner guesses the job.

O Listen. Read the information.

Virginia Clark
nurse
6:00 AM – 3:00 PM
Monday-Friday

Arthur Turner
store manager
8:00 AM – 6:00 PM
Thursday-Monday

Gregory Murphy
delivery driver
9:00 AM – 5:00 PM
Tuesday-Saturday

P Underline the *ar*, *er*, *ir*, *or*, and *ur*.

Q Listen and circle.

1. What's Virginia's job?

    a. She's a nurse.   b. Clark

2. What is Mr. Turner's first name?

    a. store manager   b. Arthur

R Choose the abbreviation.

1. Monday	(a.) M	b. W	2. Tuesday	a. Th	b. T
3. Wednesday	a. W	b. M	4. Thursday	a. T	b. Th
5. Friday	a. F	b. S	6. Saturday	a. S	b. Sun
7. Sunday	a. Sun	b. S			

S Write about your teacher.

Name:	
Title:	
Hours:	
Days:	

3 I Help Customers u

A Listen and repeat.

u   *u*   *u*   *u*

B Listen and repeat.

| **Salespeople** | **Bus drivers** | **Landscapers** | **Servers** |
| help customers. | drive buses. | cut grass and trees. | serve customers. |

C Listen and check.

	u in lunch	u in student			u in lunch	u in student
1. tube		✓	2. run			
3. flute			4. ruler			
5. duck			6. sun			
7. tuna			8. bug			

D Write *u*.

U U U U U U U U U U U U U

U

E Listen and repeat. Write *u*.

1. 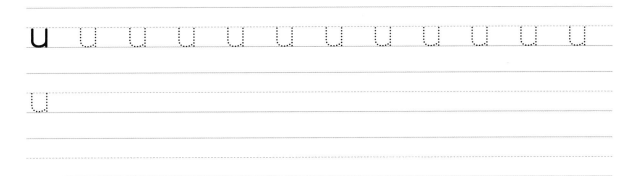 g__u__m

2. dr____m

3. b____s

4. m____g

5. c____p

6. h____g

F Say a word. Your partner writes it.

G Write *U*.

U U U U U U U U U U

U

H Listen and repeat. Write *U*.

1. **U**mbrellas are for rain.

   _____ mbrellas are for rain.

2. **U**ncle Henry is a doctor.

   _____ ncle Henry is a doctor.

I **Listen and repeat.**

A: What do you do?

B: I am a salesperson.

A: What do salespeople do?

B: We help customers.

J **Practice with** *bus driver*, *landscaper*, **and** *server*.

K **Listen and repeat.**

| but | don't | work |

A: Where do you work?

B: I'm a delivery driver.

A: Do you drive?

B: Yes, I do, but I don't drive a van.

Van

L **Practice with other students.**

M **Write** *but*, *don't*, **and** *work*.

but

don't

work

N **Spell.**

| but | don't | was | do | great | manager | write | what | please | cut | the | work |

O **Practice. Write the words on pieces of paper. Choose one. Your partner guesses the word.**

P **Listen. Track the words.**

I am a driver. I drive cars, buses, and trucks, but I don't drive motorcycles. I make deliveries to many places in Buffalo, New York. I work five days a week.

Q **Underline** *u*. **Circle** *but*, *work*, **and** *don't*.

R **Listen and circle.**

1. Does she drive motorcycles?

    a. Yes, she does.   b. No, she doesn't.

2. Where does she work?

    a. Cars, buses, and trucks.   b. Buffalo.

S **Listen. Track the words.**

I am a student. I go to school at Duggen Adult School. I listen carefully in class and help other students. My teacher is Mr. Underwood.

T **Write.**

I _____ _____ _____. I _____

_____ _____ at Duggen Adult School.

I _____ _____ carefully _____ _____

and _____ other students. My teacher is _____

_____ .

4 Please, Wear Gloves! g

A Listen and repeat.

g   g   g   g / *g   g   g   g*

B Listen and repeat.

Hotel Supervisor

7:00 AM **Get** instructions from manager.
7:15 AM **Give** instructions to your team.
1. **Greet guests.**
2. **Help with luggage.**
3. **Clean gym area.**
4. **Empty garbage.**

C Listen and check.

		g in get	g in manage
1. orange			✓
3. English	English		
5. gas			
7. angel			

		g in get	g in manage
2. green			
4. manager			
6. grapes			
8. danger			

D Write *g*. ⬚ g = g

g g g g g g g g g g g g

g

E Listen and repeat. Write *g*.

1. ba__g__   2. ____loves   3. ____lasses

4. ____iraffe   5. 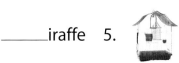 ca____e   6. 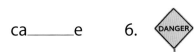 dan____er

F Write *G*.

G G G G G G G G G

G

G Listen and repeat. Write *G* and *g*.

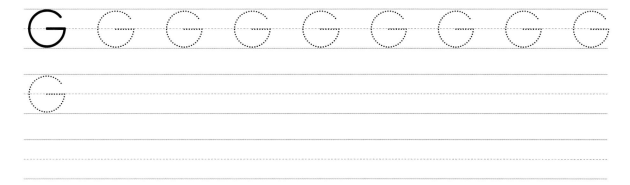

1. **G**loves are important in this job.   2. **G**ino is a **g**ood worker.

____ loves are important in this job.   ____ino is a ____ood worker.

H Listen and repeat.

Manager: Please get some glass cleaner and clean the windows.

Worker: Yes sir. It's a big job!

| big | job |

I Listen and repeat. Practice with other students.

Manager: Please get a towel and clean the counters.

Worker: Happy to. What can I do next?

Manager: Next, please clean the floors.

J Write *big* and *job*.

big

job

K Spell.

| big | job | but | don't | was | do | great | manager |
| practice | happy | please | buy | much | yes | next | |

L Practice with words from **K**.

M Listen. Track the words.

Hotel Desk Clerk

Get guest information.

Get credit card information.

Give room key to guest.

Answer questions.

guest = customer

N Underline *G* and *g*.

O Listen and circle.

1. What does the clerk do first?   a. gets information   b. asks questions

2. Where does the clerk work?   a. in the morning   b. in a hotel

P Listen. Track the words. Write.

I am a hotel clerk. I work at the Getty Hotel.
I help guests get a room. I like my job.

Q Write.

I am a _____ _____. I work at Getty Hotel.

I _____ _____ _____ _____

_____. I like my job.

5

Good Job! o

A Listen and repeat. *o* *o* *o* *o*

B Listen and repeat.

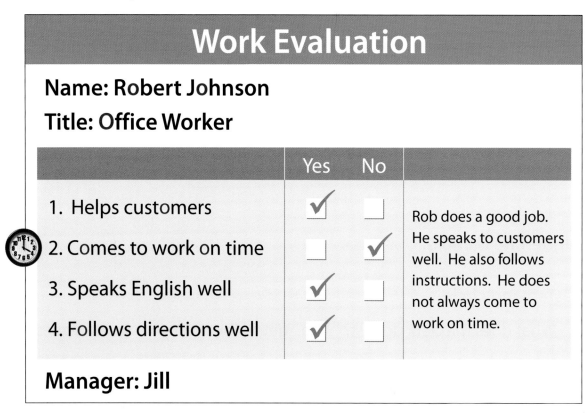

Work Evaluation

Name: Robert Johnson
Title: Office Worker

	Yes	No	
1. Helps customers	✓	☐	Rob does a good job. He speaks to customers well. He also follows instructions. He does not always come to work on time.
2. Comes to work on time	☐	✓	
3. Speaks English well	✓	☐	
4. Follows directions well	✓	☐	

Manager: Jill

C Listen and check.

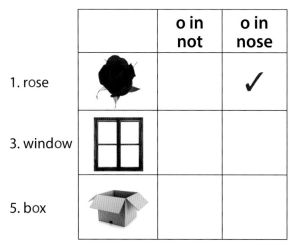

		o in not	o in nose
1. rose			✓
3. window			
5. box			

		o in not	o in nose
2. stove			
4. pot			
6. bow			

D Write o.

E Listen and repeat. Write o.

1. STOP st__o__p

2. p_____t

3. b_____x

4. _____ff

5. _____n

6. cl_____ck

F Practice. Write the words on pieces of paper. Choose one. Your partner guesses the word.

G Write O.

H Listen and repeat. Write O.

1. **O**ffice work is great work.

_____ffice work is great work.

2. I talked to **O**scar.

I talked to _____scar.

I Listen and repeat.

A: You do a good job.

B: Thank you.

J Practice with other students.

good   comes

K Listen and repeat.

A: You do a good job.

B: Thank you.

A: You need to <u>come on time</u>.

B: I'm sorry.

You need to talk to customers.

You need to come on time.

You need to practice your English.

You need to follow directions.

L Practice with other students.

M Write *good* and *comes*.

good

comes

N Spell.

good	come	big	job	but	don't	was	do	great
manager	practice	sorry	on	like	many	work	problem	need

O Say a word. Your partner writes it.

P Listen. Track the words.

> Oliver does a good job. He helps customers, but he needs to practice his English more. He is not always on time. He comes late a lot.

always = 100%

Q Underline the *o* with the sound in *not*. Circle *good* and *comes*.

R Listen and circle.

1. Oliver is a good worker.   a. true   b. false

2. Oliver always comes on time.   a. true   b. false

S Listen. Track the words.

> Otto does a good job. He helps customers, but he needs to practice his English more. He is always on time and helps customers. He also follows directions.

> Harlin does a good job. She helps customers every day. She also follows directions and comes on time. Her English is very good.

T Check.

Work Evaluation		
Name: Otto Hoffer		
	Yes	**No**
1. Helps customers		
2. Comes to work on time		
3. Speaks English well		
4. Follows directions well		

Work Evaluation		
Name: Harlin Little		
	Yes	**No**
1. Helps customers		
2. Comes to work on time		
3. Speaks English well		
4. Follows directions well		

A Circle the words.

~~great~~	x	w	i	i	j	v	w	i	l	q	n	l	y	j	w	y
manager	g	o	g	j	v	q	h	e	y	u	w	d	g	z	a	o
was	y	r	d	o	n	s	t	i	j	r	e	o	l	x	s	q
do	o	k	j	s	x	q	e	b	k	c	r	l	q	l	z	m
	u	w	o	q	c	o	i	z	p	z	c	u	d	g	o	a
but	r	q	j	k	o	n	x	u	g	d	b	u	t	j	z	n
big	w	d	o	d	m	o	p	a	r	t	r	v	g	o	b	a
job	o	k	q	f	e	t	y	d	m	s	b	i	l	b	g	g
good	c	u	u	a	c	e	z	y	a	s	r	w	p	x	r	e
	v	s	a	l	n	x	p	g	o	o	d	s	z	l	e	r
come	p	d	d	n	r	y	e	c	v	k	y	u	z	n	a	m
work	h	h	n	z	w	b	i	g	r	x	n	o	i	g	t	h

B Write the words.

great
manager
was
do
but
don't
big
job
good
come

C Write *j*.

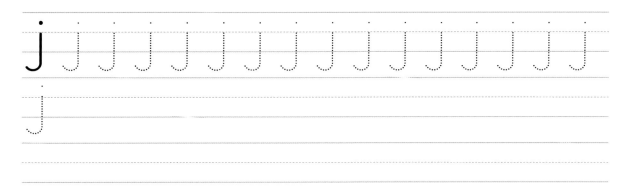

D Listen and repeat. Write *j*.

1. ___j___ob

2. _____acket

3. _____uice

4. _____et

5. _____am

6. _____ump

E Practice. Act the word out. Your partner guesses the word.

F Write *J*.

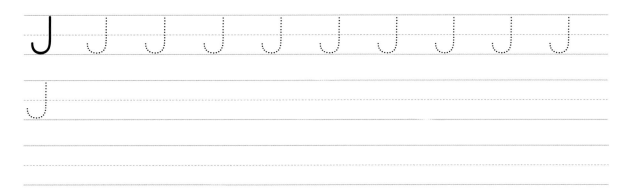

G Listen and repeat. Write *J*.

1. The teacher saw **J**im.

The teacher saw _____im.

2. **J**uly is hot.

_____uly is hot.

H **Listen and repeat.**

I	don't	drive	I don't drive a bus.
You	don't	talk	You don't talk to customers.
He She	doesn't	help serve	He doesn't help the doctor. She doesn't serve customers.
They	don't	cut	They don't cut grass.

I **Listen. Write _don't_ or _doesn't_.**

1. Jim _____ serve customers.

2. Oscar and Natalie _____ talk to customers.

3. Margarita _____ drive a bus.

4. You _____ help the doctor.

5. I _____ work.

J **Write _don't_ and _doesn't_.**

don't

doesn't

K **Spell.**

great	manager	was	do	but	don't
big	job	good	come	don't	doesn't

L Listen.

Name: Aysel Demir

Title: Office worker

Work Hours: 9AM–6PM

Days: M–F

Name: Eve Jenkins

Title: Cashier

Work Hours: 7AM–1PM

Days: M, W, F

Name: Mario Roberts

Title: Student

School Hours: 6PM–10PM

Days: M, T, W

M Write.

Name	Title	Hours	Days
Aysel			
Eve			
Mario			

N Answer the questions.

1. What does Aysel do? She is an _____.

2. What does Eve do? She is a _____.

3. What does Mario do? _____.

4. When does Aysel work? She works from _____ to _____. (hours)

5. When does Eve work? _____. (hours)

6. When does Mario go to school? He goes to school from _____ to _____. (hours)

7. Who doesn't work on Fridays? _____.

Quiz

A Listen and circle.

er 1. a.   b.   c.

or/ ur 2. a.   b.   c.

u 3. a.  b.  c.

g 4. a.  b.   c.

g 5. a.   b.   c.

o 6. a.   b.   c.

B Write.

great	job	works	comes

1. John is a manager. He has a _____ job.

2. Donna is a cashier. She has a good _____.

3. Omar is a doctor. He _____ here to the office every day.

4. Francis _____ every day for 10 hours.

C Write.

1. What time do you go to school?

   I go to school from _____.

2. What days do you go to school?

   I go to school on _____.

D Read and check.

Student Evaluation

Name: John Wesley

	Yes	No
1. Comes to school on time.	○	○
2. Helps other students.	○	○
3. Follows directions.	○	○
4. Practices English every day.	○	○

John is a good student. He listens and follows directions. He likes to help other students, and he comes on time. He practices every day.

Teacher: Mr. Abrams

E Check for you. Read to a partner.

Student Evaluation

Name: _____

	Yes	No
1. Comes to school on time.	○	○
2. Helps other students.	○	○
3. Follows directions.	○	○
4. Practices English every day.	○	○

Teacher: _____

8 Lifelong Learning

Look. Do you want to study? Do you want to get a technical degree? Do you want to go to college?

Come to Class on Time!
Review: c p s t

A **Listen and repeat.** c c cl p pr s s st t

B **Listen and repeat. Check.**

Are you a good student?

_____ I come to class every day.

_____ I come to class on time.

_____ I practice in class.

_____ I listen carefully in class.

_____ I help others in class.

_____ I practice at home.

C **Listen and circle words with the letter sound.**

c in cat 1. a.  b. c.

c in cereal 2. a.  b.  c.

p in put 3. a.  b.  c.

s in see 4. a.  b. c.

s in chairs 5. a.  b. c.

D Write the letters.

c c

d d

p p

pr pr

s s

st st

t t

nt nt

E Write sentences.

1. I come to class every day. _____

2. I come to class on time. _____

3. I practice in class. _____

4. I listen carefully in class. _____

5. I help others in class. _____

6. I practice at home. _____

F Listen and check your answers.

		Yes, I do.	No, I don't.
1.	Do you come to class every day?	☐	☐
2.	Do you come to class on time?	☐	☐
3.	Do you practice in class?	☐	☐
4.	Do you listen carefully in class?	☐	☐
5.	Do you help others in class?	☐	☐
6.	Do you practice at home?	☐	☐

G Ask four students the questions in F.

Name	1. Come to class every day	2	3	4	5	6
Mario	✗	✓	✓	✓	✓	✗

H In a group, rank 1–6.

_____ I come to class every day.　　_____ I listen carefully in class.

_____ I come to class on time.　　_____ I help others in class.

_____ I practice in class.　　_____ I practice at home.

I Spell.

> come　class　practice　on　in　at　time　yes　no　do　don't　and

J Listen. Read.

Lara is a student at Locke Adult School. She is a good student. She goes to school every day. She comes to class on time. She listens carefully and practices English a lot. She helps others in class. She doesn't practice at home.

K Listen and circle.

1. Does she practice English at home?   a. Yes, she does.   b. No, she doesn't.

2. Does she come to class on time?   a. Yes, she does.   b. No, she doesn't.

L Write sentences.

I am a student at Locke Adult School.	I am not a student at Locke Adult School.
I am a good student.	I am not a good student.
I go to school every day.	I don't go to school every day.
I come to school on time.	I don't come to school on time.
I listen carefully and practice English a lot.	I don't listen carefully and practice English a lot.
I help others in class.	I don't help others in class.
I practice at home.	I don't practice at home.

M Write sentences about you in your notebook.

2 My Study Schedule
Review: ch f l m w y

A **Listen and repeat.**   *ch   ch   f   l   m   w   y*

B **Listen and repeat.**

Schedule

	Sunday	Monday	Tuesday	Wednesday	Thursday	Friday	Saturday
9:00 am	Family Time	School	School	School	School	Study	Study
11:00 am							
12:00 pm		Work	Work	Work	Work	Work	
3:00 pm							Family Time
5:00 pm							
7:00 pm		Family Time	Family Time	Family Time	Family Time	Family Time	
9:00 pm							

C **Listen and circle the word with the letter sound.**

ch 1. a.   b.   c.

c 2. a.    b.    c.

f 3. a.    b.   c.

l 4. a.   b.   c.

w 5. a.   b.   c.

D Write the letters.

ch ch

f f

l l

m m

w w

y y

E Write sentences.

1. I go to school from 9:00 am to 12:00 pm, Monday to Thursday.

2. I work from 12:00 pm to 7:00 pm, Monday to Friday.

3. I have family time from 7:00 pm to 10:00 pm on Monday to Friday.

4. I have family time all day Sunday.

5. I have family time from 3:00 pm to 10:00 pm on Saturday.

F **Listen and repeat.**

1. Eat dinner at home.
2. Follow instructions from the boss.
3. Follow instructions from the teacher.
4. Get to work on time.
5. Help others on the job.
6. Help others learn English.
7. Listen to the teacher.
8. Play games with the children.
9. Watch TV.

G **In a group, write the items in F in the table.**

Home	School	Work
1. (Eat dinner at home.)		

H **Listen and repeat.**

A: What do you do at home?

B: I eat dinner.

A: What do you do at school?

B: I follow instructions from the teacher.

A: What do you do at work?

B: I follow instructions from my boss.

I **Practice with students.**

J **Spell.**

school   work   family   on   time   English   teacher   boss
eat   dinner   help

K **Listen and read.**

Charlie spends 33 hours a week with his family. He spends 30 hours a week at work and 21 hours a week at school.

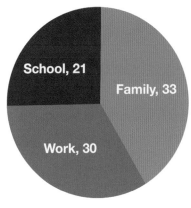

L **Listen and circle.**

1. Charlie spends more time at work than at home.   a. True   b. False
2. Charlie spends less time at school than at work.   a. True   b. False

M **Complete your schedule.**

Schedule

	Sunday	Monday	Tuesday	Wednesday	Thursday	Friday	Saturday
8:00 am							
10:00 am							
12:00 pm							
2:00 pm							
4:00 pm							
6:00 pm							
8:00 pm							
10:00 pm							

3 Can You Help Me?
Review: b l m n r y

A **Listen and repeat.** *b l m n r y*

B **Listen and repeat.**

1. community services
2. internet
3. library
4. school counselor

C **Listen and circle the words with the letter sounds.**

b 1. a. b.  c.

l 2. a. b.  c.

r 3. a. b. c.

y 4. a. b.  c.

D Write the letters.

b b

l

m m

n n

r r

y y

E Write sentences.

1. I can call community services for help.

2. I can talk to my teacher for help with the lesson.

3. I can find help at the library.

4. I can talk to a counselor for help with school.

5. I can look on the internet for information.

6. I can talk to a friend for help.

F Listen and repeat.

Student: Excuse me, can you help me?

Teacher: What can I do for you?

Student: <u>I don't understand the lesson.</u>

Teacher: OK. Let's talk.

> I don't understand the lesson.
> I need help with my classes.
> I want to find a book.
> I need to find a place to live.

G Practice with the sentences in the box.

H Check the table with a group.

Problem	Talk to a friend.	Talk to the teacher.	Go to school.	Go to the library.	Talk to a counselor.	Look on the internet.
I don't speak English.	✓	✓	✓	✓	✓	✓
I don't have a job.						
I have a question.						
I need a new class.						
I don't understand the lesson.						
I need a new apartment.						

I Spell.

> call   talk   help   with   friend   can   can't   you   need   want   like   but

J Listen. Read.

Amed needs help. He doesn't know what to do. He likes school, but his work schedule changed, and he can't go to school.

K Listen and circle.

1. Does Amed want to go to school?

   a. Yes, he does.   b. No, he doesn't.

2. Does Amed know what to do?

   a. Yes, he does.   b. No, he doesn't.

L In a group, check the three best ideas for Amed.

☐ 1. Amed can talk to his friends.

☐ 3. Amed can talk to a counselor.

☐ 5. Amed can change jobs.

☐ 7. Amed can go to another school.

☐ 2. Amed can talk to the teacher.

☐ 4. Amed can look on the internet.

☐ 6. Amed can find another class.

☐ 8. Amed can stop going to school.

M Write sentences about you.

I can

4 What's Next? *Vowels and schwa*

A Listen to the vowel sound and repeat.

a   a   e   e   i   i   o   o   u   u

B Listen and repeat.

ə   ✓   ə

com / mu / ni / ty

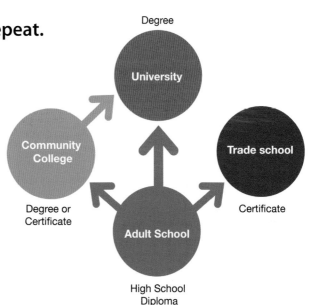

Degree

University

Community College

Trade school

Degree or Certificate

Certificate

Adult School

High School Diploma

C Listen and check.

✓

1. community	com	mu	ni	ty
2. university	u	ni	ver	si	ty
3. degree	de	gree
4. diploma	di	plo	ma
5. certificate	cer	ti	fi	cate
6. college	col	lege

D Write the letters.

a a

e e

i i

o o

u u

E Listen and repeat. Write *a*, *e*, *i*, *o*, or *u*.

1. c a t   2. s___x   3. b___g

4. b___d   5. p___t

F Listen and repeat. Write *a*, *e*, *i*, *o*, or *u*.

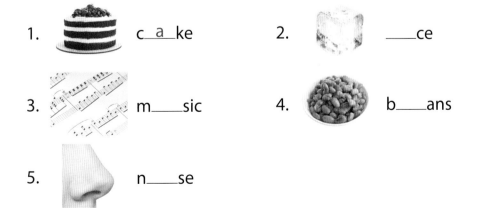

1. c a ke   2. ___ce

3. m___sic   4. b___ans

5. n___se

G **Listen and repeat. Practice.**

Counselor: Do you want to go to college?

Student: Yes, I do.

Counselor: Do you want to go to college?

Student: No, I don't. <u>I want to get a job.</u>

> I want to get a job.
> I want to go to a trade school.
> I want to go to a university.
> I want to work from home.

H **Listen and repeat.**

Counselor: Do you want to go to college?

Student: Yes, I do.

Counselor: First, you need to learn English.

Student: Yes. Then I need a high school diploma. Right?

> **then**   **right**

I **Practice with other students.**

J **Write *then* and *right*.**

then

right

K **Spell.**

> then   right   want   need   go   do   yes   first

L **Practice.**

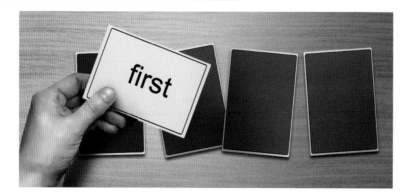

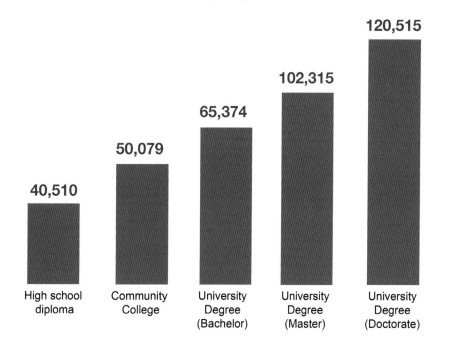

M Listen and read.

Annual Salary by Education

Bar chart values:
- High school diploma: 40,510
- Community College: 50,079
- University Degree (Bachelor): 65,374
- University Degree (Master): 102,315
- University Degree (Doctorate): 120,515

N Listen and write.

1. How much do people with Bachelor's degrees make? _____

2. How much do people with High School diplomas make? _____

O Listen.

I am a student at Lemon Adult School. I want to learn English. I also need a high school diploma. I want to go to community college. I want to be nurse.

P Copy the sentences in O.

_____

_____

_____

_____

_____

Q Write about you in your notebook.

5 My Goals! Review: c ch s sh

A Repeat.

c   c   c   ch   ch   ch   s   s   s   sh   sh   sh

B Listen and repeat.

I have a five-year plan. First, I am learning English at City College. After I learn English, I want to get a good job and help my children with school. Then I need a high school diploma. After that, I will go to trade school with my friends. I want to be a mechanic in the future.

C Listen and circle the word with the letter sound.

c in <u>c</u>ity	1. a. cat	b. face	c. chair
c in <u>c</u>ollege	2. a. car	b. center	c. teacher
ch in <u>ch</u>ildren	3. a. church	b. school	c. stomach
ch in s<u>ch</u>ool	4. a. cheese	b. mechanic	c. chips
s in <u>s</u>chool	5. a. chairs	b. music	c. sandwich
s in friend<u>s</u>	6. a. nose	b. desk	c. sandwich
sh in Engli<u>sh</u>	7. a. stomachache	b. chin	c. shirt

D Write the letters.

c c

ch ch

s s

sh sh

E Write sentences.

I have a five-year plan.

First, I am learning English at City College.

I want to get a good job and help my children with school.

Then I need a high school diploma.

After that, I will go to trade school with my friends.

I want to be a mechanic in the future.

F Listen and repeat.

A: What are your plans?

B: I am going to school.

plans	now	will

G Practice with other students.

H Listen and repeat.

A: What are your plans?

B: I am going to school right now.

A: And after that?

B: I will go to college.

Future
I will go to college.
I will get a high school diploma.
I will help my children in school.
I will go to a trade school.
I will go to a university.

I Practice. Make new conversations with sentences from the box in **H**.

J Write *plans*, *now*, and *will*.

plans

now

will

K Spell.

plans	now	will	then	right	want	need	go	do

L Practice. Play a game with the words from **K**.

M Listen. Read.

Goal

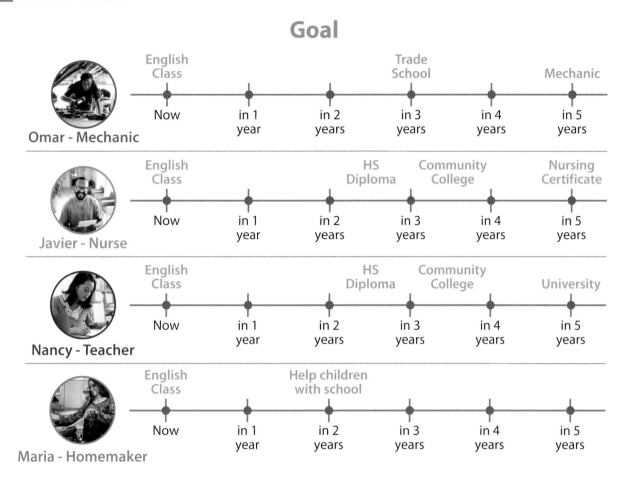

Omar - Mechanic

	Now	in 1 year	in 2 years	in 3 years	in 4 years	in 5 years
	English Class			Trade School		Mechanic

Javier - Nurse

	Now	in 1 year	in 2 years	in 3 years	in 4 years	in 5 years
	English Class			HS Diploma	Community College	Nursing Certificate

Nancy - Teacher

	Now	in 1 year	in 2 years	in 3 years	in 4 years	in 5 years
	English Class			HS Diploma	Community College	University

Maria - Homemaker

	Now	in 1 year	in 2 years	in 3 years	in 4 years	in 5 years
	English Class		Help children with school			

N Listen and circle.

1. What is Nancy's goal?

   a. She wants to go to a university.   b. She wants to get a job in three years.

2. What does Javier want to do in three years?

   a. He wants to be a nurse.   b. He wants to go to Community College.

O Write your goals.

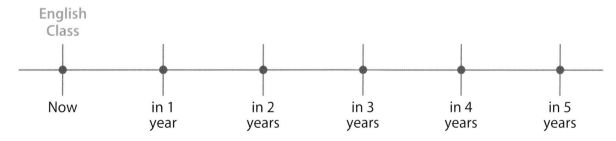

English Class

Now	in 1 year	in 2 years	in 3 years	in 4 years	in 5 years

6

Put It Together

Review *er, or / ur, u, g, o, j*

A Find and circle the words on the list.

~~call~~
English
family
help
now
talk
then
time
will
work

a	v	s	l	p	f	v	q	o	j	s	f	q	e	m	d
m	t	i	m	e	z	j	v	z	k	j	u	l	i	g	g
y	x	w	i	l	l	j	c	l	h	k	p	y	o	l	d
f	d	n	o	w	u	c	v	y	r	h	b	q	f	s	v
y	x	b	w	m	w	i	t	u	h	e	l	p	e	x	q
o	z	o	j	e	r	l	j	d	u	e	r	g	v	l	t
o	h	s	h	c	x	d	u	y	o	q	m	y	f	a	h
q	a	q	v	a	w	v	a	g	n	k	e	j	a	d	e
g	E	n	g	l	i	s	h	u	g	u	m	b	m	p	n
w	o	r	k	l	n	t	h	k	v	z	n	s	i	v	i
t	a	l	k	o	o	p	q	y	p	v	n	p	l	e	k
w	a	r	n	b	i	x	j	f	v	g	l	q	y	f	o

B Write the words.

call
English
family
help
now
talk
then
time
will
work

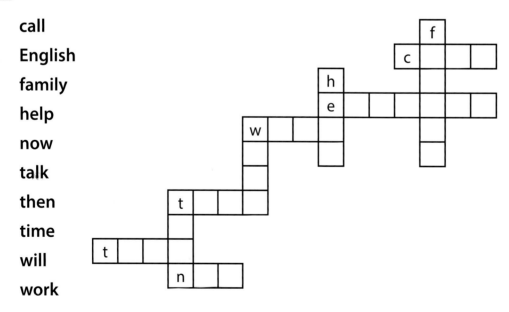

C **Write the letters and words you know.**

a a a a a a   apple   and   about

b

c

d

e

f

g

h

i

j

k

l

m

n

o

p

q

r

s

t

u

v

w

x

y

z

D Listen and repeat.

I	**come**	I come to class every day.
He She	**comes**	He comes to class every day. She comes to class every day.
I	**listen**	I listen carefully.
He She	**listens**	He listens carefully. She listens carefully.

E Write.

1. I _____ (come) to school on time.

2. Huan _____ (listen) carefully in class.

3. He _____ (help) other students.

4. I _____ (practice) English at home.

5. Silvia _____ (come) to class on time.

F Listen and repeat.

I		practice	I will practice in class.
He She	**will**	help come	He will help other students. She will come to class on time.

G Write *will*.

1. I _____ practice in class.

2. Saud _____ help other students.

3. She _____ help other students.

4. I _____ come to class on time.

5. I _____ come to class every day.

H Write your answers.

1. Where do you go to school?   I go to _____.
2. What days do you go to school?   I go to school _____.
3. What time do you come to school?   I come to school at _____.
4. Do you work, yes or no?   _____.

I Check.

Problem	Talk to a friend.	Talk to the teacher.	Go to school.	Go to the library.	Talk to a counselor.	Look on the internet.
I need help spelling a word.						
I need help with my rent.						
I want to get a high school diploma.						

J Listen. Read.

Oscar has goals. First, he will learn English. Then he will get a high school diploma. He wants to be a teacher. He needs to go to school for a long time. He will do it!

K Listen and circle.

1. What job does Oscar want?
   a. He wants to learn English.
   b. He wants to be a teacher.
   c. He wants a high school diploma.

2. What will he do first?
   a. He will get a high school diploma.
   b. He will be a teacher.
   c. He will learn English.

Quiz

A **Listen and circle.**

c in *c*ity   1. a.    b.   c.

c in *c*ollege   2. a.   b.   c.

ch in *ch*ildren   3. a.   b.   c.

ch in s*ch*ool   4. a.    b.   c.

b   5. a.   b.    c.

l   6. a.   b.    c.

f   7. a.   b.   c.

B **Write the letter to complete the word.**

1. I l___ke bananas.

2. We need to pr___ctice our English.

3. She c___mes to school every day.

4. Do you have a stomachache? No, I d___n't.

5. They c___n get a high school diploma.

6. I am learning Engl___sh.

7. We n___ed to learn English.

8. He needs h___lp.

9. I eat l___nch at 12:00 pm.

10. I want to go to a ___niversity.

C **Read and circle.**

Marco's Schedule

	Sunday	Monday	Tuesday	Wednesday	Thursday	Friday	Saturday
9:00 am	Family Time	Study	Study	Study	Study	Study	Family Time
11:00 am		Work	Work	Work	Work	Work	
12:00 pm							
3:00 pm							
5:00 pm							
7:00 pm		School	School	School	School	Family Time	
9:00 pm							

1. What time does he start to study?

   a. 9:00 am b. 12:00 am c. 7:00 pm

2. What days does he go to work?

   a. Monday, Tuesday, Wednesday, Thursday
   b. Monday–Friday
   c. Sunday

3. What days does he go to school?

   a. Monday, Tuesday, Wednesday, Thursday
   b. Monday–Friday
   c. Sunday

Review 1

A **Listen to the letter names then repeat.**

a b c ch d e f h k l m n p r s sh t w y

B **Listen to the letter sounds then repeat.**

a b c ch d e f h k l m n p r s sh t w y

C **Write.**

a _____   m _____

b _____   n _____

c _____   p _____

d _____   r _____

e _____   s _____

f _____   t _____

h _____   w _____

k _____   y _____

l _____   _____

D Write. Ask a partner.

Please spell your first name. _____

Please spell your last name. _____

E Write. Ask a partner.

Where are you from?

Please spell it. _____

F Write. Ask a partner.

Where do you live (city)?

Please spell it. _____

G Write. Ask a partner.

What is your phone number? _____

H Write.

1. My name is _____.

2. My last name is _____.

3. I am from _____.

4. I live in _____.

5. My phone number is _____.

A **Read.**

I am Alberto Suarez. I want to rent an apartment. I need a two-bedroom home with two bathrooms. I want to live in Texas.

B **What apartment is for Alberto? Circle.**

#1	#2	#3
For Rent	**For Rent**	**For Rent**
Bedroom: 3	**Bedroom:** 2	**Bedroom:** 2
Bathrooms: 2	**Bathrooms:** 2	**Bathrooms:** 1
City: Los Angeles	**City:** Dallas	**City:** Austin
State: California	**State:** Texas	**State:** Texas
Call: 213-555-2223	**Call:** 972-555-6325	**Call:** 512-555-4712

C **Complete the chart with information from B.**

House	Bedrooms	Bathrooms	City, State	Phone
House #1				
House #2				
House #3				

D **Read.**

Amina is sick. She has the flu with a headache and a stomachache. She needs to go to the doctor. She doesn't know what medicine to take.

E **Read.**

Pain Reliever

Instructions: Take two capsules every four hours if needed. Do not take more than eight capsules in 24 hours.

Antacid

Instructions: Take two tablets every four hours. Do not take more than eight tablets in 24 hours.

F Write.

Medicine	Capsule / Syrup / Tablet	How Many?	Every ____ Hours
Pain Reliever			
Antacid			

G Read.

    Kai goes to Academy Adult School. He wants to be an architect. He wants to go to a community college. First, he needs to learn more English and then he wants to get a high school diploma. Right now, he is a delivery person.

H Circle the correct answers.

1. What job does Kai want in the future?

   a. delivery person   b. student   c. architect

2. What does Kai do now?

   a. delivery person   b. architect   c. student

3. What does Kai want?

   a. high school   b. community   c. adult school
       diploma   college

I Write. When can Kai study?

1. Kai can study on _____ from _____ to _____.

2. Kai can study on _____ from _____ to 9 pm.

	Sunday	Monday	Tuesday	Wednesday	Thursday	Friday	Saturday
8:00 am	Family						Family
10:00 am							
12:00 am			Work	Work	Work	Work	
2:00 pm							
4:00 pm							
6:00 pm		School	School	School	School		
8:00 pm							

Writing Practice

Alphabet

A a

B b

C c

D d

E e

F f

G g

H h

I i

J j

K k

L l

M m

N n

O o

P p

Q q

R r

S s

T t

U u

V v

W w

X x

Y y

Z z

Word Practice

name	this
happy	live
where	first
what	last
from	

friend	my
please	your
on	go
in	school
at	you

buy	need
like	and
want	cook
eat	cut
meal	for

UNIT 4

too	many
red	small
blue	large
black	the
how	wearing

Word Practice

UNIT 5

corner	right
of	by
turn	work
left	yes
no	have
with	has

UNIT 6

day	who
week	next
maybe	some
feel	take
can't	am

later   are

problem   is

UNIT 7

great   do

manager   but

was   work

big   doesn't

job   don't

good

comes

Word Practice

then

right

plans

now

will

Credits

Credits

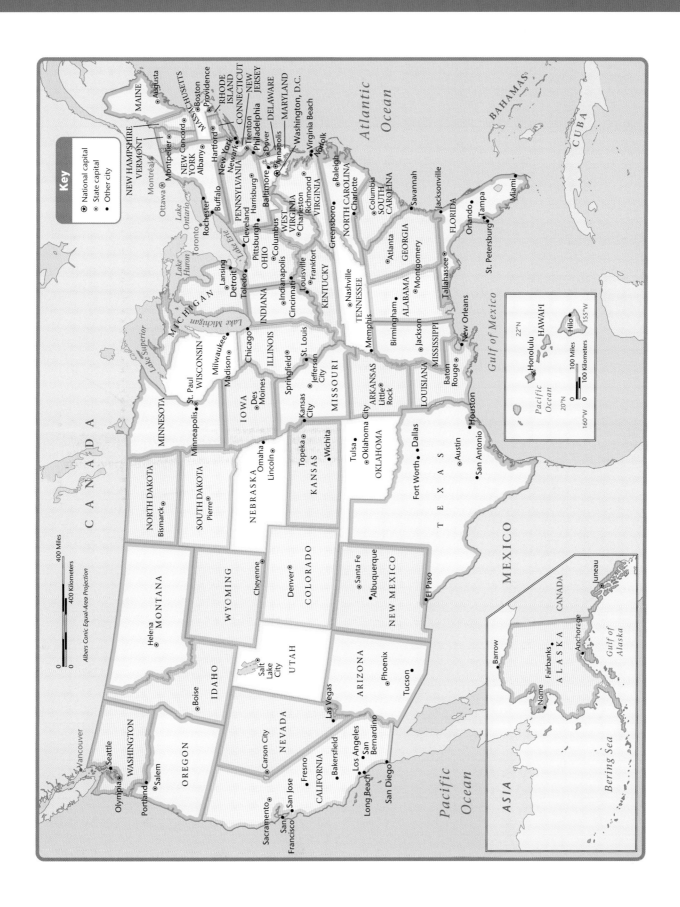

Notes

Notes

Notes